*in all shakespeare's

Act 1 = intro
Act 2 = plot in action
Act 3 = Climax
Act 4 = falling action
Act 5 = Rsolution (AKA everyone dies).

THE TEMPEST

* when sighting =>
II i, V iii etc.
Roman numeral + i's

Molly.

HBJ SHAKESPEARE

THE TEMPEST

edited by
Allan Patenaude

Harcourt Brace Jovanovich, Canada

Toronto Orlando San Diego London Sydney

Harbrace Shakespeare: Series Editor, Ken Roy

Canadian Cataloguing in Publication Data

Shakespeare, William, 1564–1616
  The Tempest

(Harbrace Shakespeare)
For use in high schools
ISBN 0–7747–1359–3

I. Patenaude, Allan   II. Title.   III. Series.

PR2833.A2P3 1990   822.3'3   C90-093253-8

98 99 00 01 02   6 5 4 3 2

Editorial Director: Murray Lamb
Senior Editor: Lydia Fletcher
Project Editor: Sharon Jennings
Project Coordinator: Susan McCafferty
Production Editors: Susan Skivington
     and Susan Marshall
Designer: Michael van Elsen
Illustrators: Marika and Laszlo Gal
Cover Illustrators: Marika and Laszlo Gal
Typesetter: Q Composition
Printed in Canada by Friesen Printers

Acknowledgments

The editor and publisher acknowledge the consultants listed below for their contributions to the development of this program:

Denise Cummings
English Department Head, Wagar High School, The Protestant School Board of Greater Montreal, Montreal, Quebec

Grace Y.K. Fatkin
Former Secondary English Teacher, Langley District School Board, Langley, British Columbia

To the Reader

In many ways, *The Tempest* is a fairy tale. The narrative that unfolds has all the required ingredients: an enchanted island setting, a beautiful young daughter of a duke and a handsome prince. Also included are a king, several villains, a demi-monster and a fairy-like spirit. Nymphs, goddesses, and several strange shapes help to tell the story as well, and create its spellbinding atmosphere. In *The Tempest* magic of both black and white varieties works its powers on the characters, and sometimes on us, the participating audience.

Although fairy tales may appear to be simple in their meaning, they are not always so. As you experience the conflicting forces of good and evil struggle against each other in *The Tempest*, you may find yourself thinking about the real world and the people who inhabit it.

This edition of *The Tempest* encourages you to participate actively in the experience of the play and to consider your thoughts and feelings about the experience. Some of the activities which follow the scenes and acts invite you to build upon your responses to the play's events by sharing your opinions with others. Some activities encourage you to collaborate with other students in the preparation of performances, displays, and written and oral presentations. Other ones invite you to complete tasks on your own. As you complete these activities you will probably find that you are shaping and building your own sense of the play, and the themes and issues it presents.

Before you begin *The Tempest*, read and discuss the questions in the "Getting Started" activities that follow. They offer you an opportunity to explore some of the situations and theme topics you will encounter as you experience the play.

Getting Started

Before you explore the drama of *The Tempest*, you may wish to discuss some of the questions and themes presented in this play. This will give you a good opportunity to begin writing in your journal. Record what you think are some of the important and interesting points that were made in your discussions. These thoughts and opinions will become reference points for you as you select activities to complete that follow the various scenes and acts in this play. You may wish to return to them and expand upon some of your ideas as you explore the play.

1. In a group, brainstorm a list of ideas you have about the title of the play. What comes to your mind when you think of a tempest? What are some of the effects that tempests can have? The root of the word "tempest" is the Latin word, tempestas, meaning time. What does this definition contribute to your sense of the title?

2. Examine the cover illustration and the ones that appear throughout the text. See if you can match the characters who appear in these illustrations to the characters that appear in the list on page 5. In a group, discuss your responses to the following questions:
   • What might these characters be like?
   • What might they do during the course of the play?
   • What other clues do the illustrations suggest about the content of the play?

   Keep a record of your responses in a journal. As you experience the play, you may wish to expand your initial ideas.

3. Imagine that you are required to spend the next three years of your life on a remote island completely out of touch with civilization. Make a list of personal possessions you would take with you. Remember your choices will have to satisfy your physical, intellectual, and emotional needs. Share your list with classmates.

4. In a group recall stories you have read and/or films, TV shows you have seen in which people undertook journeys for specific purposes. What were some of their reasons? What kinds of obstacles did they encounter?

How would you define a spiritual journey? What might prompt someone to undertake such a journey?

5. Imagine a group of people who didn't know one another were stranded on a deserted island in the middle of the ocean, and were likely going to be there for a long time.
   - How might they choose to govern themselves?
   - What might be the outcome of their experience?

   Write your ideas in a journal entry.

6. Do you think that there are people who are just born evil, or do you believe that some people become evil because of events that occur in their lives? What should be done with those who are either evil by birth or who become evil?

7. Young people usually see the world differently from adults. In a group, identify some of these differences. What do you think happens to the young peoples' perspectives of the world when they "grow up"?

8. Recall experiences you have had or stories you know in which a person who was wronged had to decide between seeking revenge or offering forgiveness. How did the person reach his or her decision? What was the final outcome? Record in a journal entry whether you agree or disagree with the decision and explain your opinion.

9. With a group brainstorm a list of as many current political leaders as you can who have been deposed by their people. Generally, what do you think caused the uprisings? What replaced authoritarian rule? How successful do you think the new forms of government have been or will be?

Dramatis Personae

(Characters in the Play)

Alonso, King of Naples
Sebastian, his brother
Prospero, the right Duke of Milan
Miranda, daughter to Prospero
Ariel, an airy spirit
Antonio, his brother, the usurping Duke of Milan
Ferdinand, son to the King of Naples
Gonzalo, an honest old counsellor
Adrian
Francisco } lords
Caliban, a savage and deformed slave
Trinculo, a jester
Stephano, a drunken butler
Master of a ship
Boatswain
Mariners
Iris
Ceres
Juno } presented by spirits
Nymphs
Reapers
Other spirits attending on Prospero
Scene: A ship at sea; an uninhabited island

Act 1, Scene 1

In this scene . . .

The play opens on board a ship that is being tossed by a raging storm. The Master and Boatswain attempt to save the ship, but they and the crew are hindered by the interference of the royal passengers on board. These passengers refuse to return to their cabins and annoy and taunt the sailors. The scene ends as the ship splits apart, and all on board appear to be doomed.

Stage direction – *Shipmaster:* the captain of a ship in charge of navigation

1   *Boatswain:* a petty office in charge of a ship's crew, anchors and rigging, and who conveys the captain's commands to the crew

2   *what cheer?:* What is the condition of the ship?

3   *Good:* my good man; *fall to't, yarely:* move and act quickly

4   *bestir:* move briskly

5   *my hearts:* my lads, my sailors

7-8   *Blow, till . . . enough:* The boatswain addresses the wind as if it were a man with distended cheeks. He does not fear the force of the wind as long as there is open sea in which to manoeuvre the vessel safely.

10   *Play the men:* Act like brave men.

13   *You mar our labour:* You are hindering us in our efforts to save the ship.

14   *you do assist the storm:* You are making the situation worse.

16   *Hence:* Away; *roarers:* blustering winds

20-21   *You are a/counsellor:* You are a man in authority.

22   *work the . . . present:* calm the sea and the wind

23   *hand:* handle

24-26   *make/yourself . . . hap:* Prepare yourselves to face death if it should soon happen.

Act 1, Scene 1

*On a ship at sea: a tempestuous
noise of thunder and lightning
heard.*

*Enter a Shipmaster and a
Boatswain.*

✱ They're drawing...

Master: Boatswain!

Boatswain: Here, master: what cheer?

Master: Good, speak to the mariners: fall to't, yarely, or
we run ourselves aground: bestir, bestir.   [*Exit.*]

[*Enter Mariners.*]

Boatswain: Heigh, my hearts! Cheerly, cheerly, my hearts!   5
yare, yare! Take in the topsail. Tend to the master's
whistle. Blow, till thou burst thy wind, if room
enough!

[*Enter Alonso, Sebastian, Antonio, Ferdinand, Gonzalo,
and others.*]

Alonso: Good boatswain, have care. Where's the master?
Play the men.   10

Boatswain: I pray now, keep below.

Antonio: Where is the master, boatswain?

Boatswain: Do you not hear him? You mar our labour: keep
your cabins: you do assist the storm.

Gonzalo: Nay, good, be patient.   15

Boatswain: When the sea is. Hence! What cares these roarers
for the name of king? To cabin: silence! Trouble us
not.

Gonzalo: Good, yet remember whom thou hast aboard.

Boatswain: None that I more love than myself. You are a   20
counsellor; if you can command these elements to
silence, and work the peace of the present, we will
not hand a rope more; use your authority: if you cannot, give thanks you have lived so long, and make
yourself ready in your cabin for the mischance of the   25

✱ poor people = not iambic pentameter
b/ of a status thing. → they use
free verse.

29-30   *no drowning mark . . . gallows:* This phrase refers to the proverb, "He who is born to be hanged need fear no drown-
ing." In other words, the boatswain appears to Gonzalo as a
man destined to experience death by hanging and not by
drowning.

35   *Bring/her . . . main-course:* Try to steer the ship towards the
open sea by means of using the largest sail of the ship.
(The wind is forcing the ship ashore.)

37   *our office:* the duties that we as sailors have to perform

38   *give o'er:* abandon our efforts to save the ship

42   *Work you then:* Do the work yourselves.

43   *cur:* dog; *whoreson:* bastard

46   *I'll warrant him for drowning:* I'd guarantee he's not destined
to die by drowning.

48   *unstanched:* wide open; *unstanched wench:* an obscene
reference to a promiscuous woman

49-50   *Lay her . . . her off:* The ship is still being forced closer to the
shore; the boatswain orders that both the mainsail and the
foresail be used to move the ship towards the open sea.

52   *must our mouths be cold?:* Must we die?

55   *merely:* completely

56   *wide-chapp'd rascal:* big-mouthed villain

57   *The washing of ten tides:* while the tide ebbs and flows ten
times; i.e., five days. This is a reference to the practice of
hanging pirates on the shore and leaving their bodies there
until three tides had washed over them.

59   *And gape . . . him:* as though the sea opens itself as wide as
possible to swallow him

hour, if it so hap. Cheerly, good hearts! Out of our
way, I say.   [*Exit.*]

Gonzalo: I have great comfort from this fellow: methinks
he hath no drowning mark upon him; his complexion
is perfect gallows. Stand fast, good Fate, to his hang-   30
ing: make the rope of his destiny our cable, for our own
doth little advantage. If he be not born to be hanged,
our case is miserable.   [*Exeunt.*]
[*Re-enter Boatswain.*]

Boatswain: Down with the topmast! Yare! Lower, lower!
Bring her to try with main-course. [*A cry within.*] A   35
plague upon this howling! they are louder than the
weather or our office.
[*Re-enter Sebastian, Antonio, and Gonzalo.*]
Yet again! what do you here? Shall we give o'er and
drown? Have you a mind to sink?

Sebastian: A plague o' your throat, you bawling, blasphe-   40
mous, incharitable dog!

Boatswain: Work you then.

Antonio: Hang, cur! Hang, you whoreson insolent
noisemaker! We are less afraid to be drowned than
thou art.   45

Gonzalo: I'll warrant him for drowning; though the ship
were no stronger than a nutshell, and as leaky as an
unstanched wench.

Boatswain: Lay her a-hold, a-hold! Set her two courses; off
to sea again; lay her off.   50
[*Enter Mariners wet.*]

Mariners: All lost! To prayers, to prayers! All lost!

Boatswain: What, must our mouths be cold?

Gonzalo: The king and prince at prayers! Let's assist them,
For our case is as theirs.

Sebastian: I'm out of patience.

Antonio: We are merely cheated of our lives by drunkards: 55
This wide-chapp'd rascal—would thou mightst lie
drowning
The washing of ten tides!

Gonzalo: He'll be hang'd yet,
Though every drop of water swear against it,
And gape at widest to glut him.

67   *ling:* heather; *broom:* a yellow shrub plant; *furze:* a prickly
      bush

68-69 *fain die/a dry death:* I would much rather die by some other
       way than by drowning.

[*A confused noise within:*   "Mercy on us!"—   60
  "We split, we split!"—"Farewell, my wife and
  children!"—"Farewell, brother!"—"We split,
  we split, we split!"]
Antonio: Let's all sink with the king.
Sebastian: Let's take leave of him.   65
                    [*Exeunt Antonio and Sebastian.*]
Gonzalo: Now would I give a thousand furlongs of sea for
  an acre of barren ground, ling, heath, broom, furze, any
  thing. The wills above be done! But I would fain die
  a dry death.   [*Exeunt.*]

Act 1, Scene 1: Activities

1. If you were the Boatswain (the officer in charge of summoning men to duty) and could write a letter to the owner of the boat about the behaviour of the passengers on this trip, what would you say? What observations would you make to the owner about the passengers being political leaders? Share your letter with others in a group.

2. In a group, discuss how you would stage the violence of the tempest and the confusion on the ship. Reread the stage directions provided in this scene. Then consider the following:

   a) How would you use lighting and sound to create the desired effect?

   b) How would you have the actors move to give the impression they were on board a ship during a storm? Share your ideas. If a stage is available, rehearse and present the scene or a scene segment to your classmates.

3. In Act 1, Scene 2, we learn that other ships in the fleet survived the tempest and continued their journey to Naples. Working with a partner, assume that one of you is a passenger who witnessed the events of Scene 1 from the deck of another ship. The other partner is a reporter, who interviews the passenger on his/her return to Naples. Present the interview to classmates as "live coverage" for a TV newscast. You might prefer, instead, to write the interview as a newspaper story.

4. Reread the speeches that Gonzalo makes in this scene and compare them with the speeches made by Alonso, Antonio, and Sebastian. In a journal, record your impressions of Gonzalo and the three other regal passengers based on their speeches. Would you want one or more of them as a friend? Explain.

For this next scene . . .

Imagine you are in a situation where you could invent and tell others anything about yourself that you wanted to tell, including circumstances about your birth and family background. Record what you would say as a journal entry. Later, you may wish to use your entry to develop a short biography or autobiography.

Act 1, Scene 2

In this scene . . .

On the island, Miranda is very distressed by the ship-wreck she has just witnessed. Prospero tells her that, with his magical powers, he caused the tempest, and kept the ship's passengers safe at the same time. He then proceeds to tell Miranda the history of their lives. In the course of his tale, he explains the circumstances and events which led to their being expelled from their native Milan, cast adrift in an old boat, and finally washed ashore on the island where they now live. He tells Miranda that this tempest has now brought to their shores the enemies from 12 years ago who overthrew him. He then puts Miranda into an enchanted sleep and summons Ariel, a spirit under his control. Ariel describes to Prospero how he created the tempest according to Prospero's wishes. Prospero is satisfied but reminds Ariel that there is still more to be done before the day is over. Ariel responds by complaining about being Prospero's slave. The complaint prompts Prospero to remind Ariel that it was he (Prospero) who released Ariel from a spell placed on him by the witch Sycorax who once ruled the island.

After Ariel departs, Prospero wakens Miranda and together they visit Caliban, their servant. Caliban is the half-human, half-monster son of Sycorax. He enters cursing both Miranda and Prospero for the life he lives under Prospero's control. After Prospero reminds Caliban of the circumstances which have lead to his foul and menial existence, Caliban departs.

Ariel appears again, this time with Ferdinand, the son of the King of Naples. He believes his father has drowned in the storm. However, when Ferdinand sees Miranda, his sorrow lessens and the two fall in love at first sight.

Stage direction – *cell:* a small humble abode such as a cave or humble dwelling

1	*by your art:* by your magical power
2	*allay:* calm
3	*stinking pitch:* foul, black, and sticky substance, and is the residue distilled from tar or turpentine; it is semi-liquid when hot
4-5	*But that . . . out:* The winds caused the waves of the sea to rise so high that their waters quenched the fires in the skies ("welkin's cheek") that were melting the pitch.
6	*brave:* gallant, fine
11	*or ere:* before, rather than
13	*The fraughting souls within her:* the passengers who were the ship's freight; *Be collected:* be calm
14	*amazement:* astonishment, bewilderment
19	*Of whence:* from where
19-20	*more better/ . . . cell:* greater in social position and origin than simply the master of this humble dwelling. The use of the double comparative "more better" was common in Elizabethan English.
22	*meddle:* mingle

Scene 2

The island. Before Prospero's cell.

Enter Prospero and Miranda.

Miranda: If by your art, my dearest father, you have
  Put the wild waters in this roar, allay them.
  The sky, it seems, would pour down stinking pitch,
  But that the sea, mounting to the welkin's cheek,
  Dashes the fire out. O, I have suffer'd   5
  With those that I saw suffer! A brave vessel,
  Who had, no doubt, some noble creature in her,
  Dash'd all to pieces. O, the cry did knock
  Against my very heart! Poor souls, they perish'd!
  Had I been any god of power, I would   10
  Have sunk the sea within the earth, or ere
  It should the good ship so have swallow'd and
  The fraughting souls within her.
Prospero: Be collected:
  No more amazement: tell your piteous heart
  There's no harm done.
Miranda: O, woe the day!
Prospero: No harm.   15
  I have done nothing but in care of thee,
  Of thee, my dear one, thee, my daughter, who
  Art ignorant of what thou art, nought knowing
  Of whence I am, nor that I am more better
  Than Prospero, master of a full poor cell,   20
  And thy no greater father.
Miranda: More to know
  Did never meddle with my thoughts.
Prospero: 'Tis time
  I should inform thee farther. Lend thy hand,
  And pluck my magic garment from me.—So:
                    [*Lays down his mantle.*]
  Lie there, my art. Wipe thou thine eyes; have comfort.   25

26   *direful:* terrible

30   *perdition:* loss

31   *Betid:* happened

33   *farther:* more

35   *bootless inquisition:* questions for which no answers were
        provided

41   *Out:* yet

45-46   *And rather . . . warrants:* a vague memory of events which I
        can't recall in detail

50   *backward and abysm of time?:* the far-reaching depths of the
        past

51   *aught ere:* anything before

53   *since:* ago

The direful spectacle of the wreck, which touch'd
The very virtue of compassion in thee,
I have with such provision in mine art
So safely order'd, that there is no soul,
No, not so much perdition as an hair   30
Betid to any creature in the vessel
Which thou heard'st cry, which thou saw'st sink.
   Sit down;
For thou must now know farther.
Miranda: You have often
Begun to tell me what I am; but stopp'd
And left me to a bootless inquisition,   35
Concluding "Stay: not yet".
Prospero: The hour's now come;
The very minute bids thee ope thine ear;
Obey and be attentive. Canst thou remember
A time before we came unto this cell?
I do not think thou canst, for then thou wast not   40
Out three years old.
Miranda: Certainly, sir, I can.
Prospero: By what? By any other house or person?
Of any thing the image tell me, that
Hath kept with thy remembrance.
Miranda: 'Tis far off,
And rather like a dream than an assurance   45
That my remembrance warrants. Had I not
Four or five women once that tended me?
Prospero: Thou hadst, and more, Miranda. But how is it
That this lives in thy mind? What seest thou else
In the dark backward and abysm of time?   50
If thou remember'st aught ere thou camest here,
How thou camest here thou mayst.
Miranda: But that I do not.
Prospero: Twelve year since, Miranda, twelve year since,
Thy father was the Duke of Milan, and
A prince of power.
Miranda: Sir, are not you my father?   55
Prospero: Thy mother was a piece of virtue, and
She said thou wast my daughter; and thy father
Was Duke of Milan; and his only heir

59   *no worse issued:* born of no less humble a father than that of the Duke of Milan

61   *Or blessed was't we did?:* Or was it a blessing that we did leave Milan?

62   *heaved thence:* cast out

63   *holp:* help

64-65   *teen that . . . remembrance:* the trouble I have caused you but of which I cannot remember

68   *perfidious:* treacherous, distrustful

70   *manage:* management

71   *signories:* lordships, high-ranking positions in government

72   *prime duke:* first among all the dukes

74   *parallel:* Milan was considered to be the principal dukedom in Europe; therefore, Prospero was considered to be a noble-man who had no equal in terms of his position and dignity.

76-77   *transported/And rapt:* so filled with joy arising from my studies

80   *who to advance:* who to promote

81   *To trash for over-topping:* who to prevent from becoming too powerful

81-83   *new created . . . form'd 'em:* Antonio rearranged Prospero's appointed cabinet in such a way that he could control the affairs of state in accordance with his own personal ambitions and goals.

85-87   *he was . . . out on't:* Antonio is like the ivy which saps the life or greenness from a tree trunk.

92   *O'er-prized all popular rate:* Prospero valued his studies more than the honour and respect he received as Duke of Milan.

93-94   *my trust/Like a good parent:* Just like a good father can pro-duce a wicked son, my trust led to falsehood.

A princess, no worse issued.
Miranda: O the heavens!
  What foul play had we, that we came from thence?   60
  Or blessed was't we did?
Prospero: Both, both, my girl:
  By foul play, as thou say'st, were we heaved thence,
  But blessedly holp hither.
Miranda: O, my heart bleeds
  To think o' the teen that I have turn'd you to,
  Which is from my remembrance! Please you, farther.   65
Prospero: My brother and thy uncle, call'd Antonio—
  I pray thee, mark me—that a brother should
  Be so perfidious!—he whom, next thyself,
  Of all the world I loved, and to him put
  The manage of my state; as at that time   70
  Through all the signories it was the first,
  And Prospero the prime duke, being so reputed
  In dignity, and for the liberal arts
  Without a parallel; those being all my study,
  The government I cast upon my brother,   75
  And to my state grew stranger, being transported
  And rapt in secret studies. Thy false uncle—
  Dost thou attend me?
Miranda: Sir, most heedfully.
Prospero: Being once perfected how to grant suits,
  How to deny them, who to advance, and who   80
  To trash for over-topping, new created
  The creatures that were mine, I say, or changed 'em,
  Or else new form'd 'em; having both the key
  Of officer and office, set all hearts i' the state
  To what tune pleased his ear; that now he was   85
  The ivy which had hid my princely trunk,
  And suck'd my verdure out on't. Thou attend'st not.
Miranda: O, good sir, I do.
Prospero: I pray thee, mark me.
  I, thus neglecting worldly ends, all dedicated
  To closeness and the bettering of my mind   90
  With that which, but by being so retired,
  O'er-prized all popular rate, in my false brother
  Awaked an evil nature; and my trust,

97   *confidence sans bound:* Prospero had complete trust in Antonio.

99   *But what . . . exact:* Antonio took advantage not only of Prospero's legal tax revenues, but also enforced illegal taxes from the Duke's subjects.

99-102   *like one/ . . . lie:* like a person who becomes so used to lying that he comes to believe the lies he tells are true

103-105   *out o' the . . . prerogative:* While substituting as Duke for Prospero, Antonio acted as though he were the real Duke with all the power of the position.

107-109   *To have . . . Milan:* Antonio wanted to turn his role as the duke's agent into a position in which he was indeed the real duke.

110   *temporal royalties:* worldly power

111   *confederates:* enters into an arrangement with

112   *dry:* thirsty; *dry he was for sway:* so longing for the power of governing

114   *Subject his . . . crown:* placed his own crown as a duke under the higher crown of the King of Naples

117   *his condition and the event:* the position of inferiority in which Antonio had placed himself and Milan by his agreement with the King of Naples and the event that took place as a result of it

120   *Good wombs . . . sons:* good parents have produced wicked children. (This lines echoes Prospero's words, "Like a good parent," in line 94.)

122   *inveterate:* of long stand and unchangeable; *suit:* petition or proposal

123   *in lieu o' the premises:* in return for the conditions Antonio had made

125   *extirpate:* destroy

128   *levied:* raised or gathered

Like a good parent, did beget of him
A falsehood in its contrary, as great   95
As my trust was; which had indeed no limit,
A confidence sans bound. He being thus lorded,
Not only with what my revenue yielded,
But what my power might else exact, like one
Who having into truth, by telling of it,   100
Made such a sinner of his memory,
To credit his own lie, he did believe
He was indeed the duke; out o' the substitution,
And executing the outward face of royalty,
With all prerogative:—hence his ambition growing,   105
—Dost thou hear?
Miranda: Your tale, sir, would cure deafness.
Prospero: To have no screen between this part he play'd
    And him he play'd it for, he needs will be
    Absolute Milan. Me, poor man, my library
    Was dukedom large enough: of temporal royalties   110
    He thinks me now incapable; confederates,
    So dry he was for sway, wi' the King of Naples
    To give him annual tribute, do him homage,
    Subject his coronet to his crown, and bend
    The dukedom yet unbow'd,—alas, poor Milan!—   115
    To most ignoble stooping.
Miranda: O the heavens!
Prospero: Mark his condition and the event; then tell me
    If this might be a brother.
Miranda: I should sin
    To think but nobly of my grandmother:
    Good wombs have borne bad sons.
Prospero: Now the condition.   120
    This King of Naples, being an enemy
    To me inveterate, hearkens my brother's suit;
    Which was, that he, in lieu o' the premises
    Of homage and I know not how much tribute,
    Should presently extirpate me and mine   125
    Out of the dukedom, and confer fair Milan,
    With all the honours, on my brother: whereon,
    A treacherous army levied, one midnight
    Fated to the purpose, did Antonio open

131   *thence:* i.e., into that dead of darkness

134-135 *hint/That . . . to't:* It is a story that makes me want to cry.

137   *Which now's upon's:* which are now happening

138   *impertinent:* inappropriate or pointless

139   *wench:* Here the word signifies a young and innocent girl, especially a peasant girl. It has a very different meaning than in "unstanched wench," Scene 1, line 46.

140   *durst not:* dare not

143   *foul ends:* wicked purposes

146   *butt:* a boat that is hardly seaworthy

151   *but loving wrong:* discomfort or injury without any wrong or harmful intentions

152   *cherubin:* an angel usually portrayed as a chubby, rosy-faced child

155-156 *deck'd the . . . groan'd:* cried tears into the sea as a result of my heavy sorrow

157   *An undergoing stomach:* the courage to endure

158   *ensue:* follow

The gates of Milan; and, i' the dead of darkness, 130
The ministers for the purpose hurried thence
Me and thy crying self.
Miranda: Alack, for pity!
I, not remembering how I cried out then,
Will cry it o'er again: it is a hint
That wrings mine eyes to't.
Prospero: Hear a little further, 135
And then I'll bring thee to the present business
Which now's upon's; without the which, this story
Were most impertinent.
Miranda: Wherefore did they not
That hour destroy us?
Prospero: Well demanded, wench:
My tale provokes that question. Dear, they durst not, 140
So dear the love my people bore me; nor set
A mark so bloody on the business; but
With colours fairer painted their foul ends.
In few, they hurried us aboard a bark,
Bore us some leagues to sea; where they prepared 145
A rotten carcass of a butt, not rigg'd,
Nor tackle, sail, nor mast; the very rats
Instinctively have quit it: there they hoist us,
To cry to the sea that roar'd to us; to sigh
To the winds, whose pity, sighing back again, 150
Did us but loving wrong.
Miranda: Alack, what trouble
Was I then to you!
Prospero: O, a cherubin
Thou wast that did preserve me. Thou didst smile,
Infused with a fortitude from heaven,
When I have deck'd the sea with drops full salt, 155
Under my burthen groan'd; which raised in me
An undergoing stomach, to bear up
Against what should ensue.
Miranda: How came we ashore?
Prospero: By Providence divine.
Some food we had and some fresh water, that 160
A noble Neapolitan, Gonzalo,
Out of his charity, who being then appointed

163   *Master of this design:* the person in charge of the whole operation

165   *Which since have steaded much:* which have since held up and been useful to us

172   *more profit:* benefit

174   *For vainer hours:* for less profitable activities

177   *Know thus far forth:* Prospero will tell Miranda a little more of the story.

179   *Now my dear lady:* Fortune is now a friend and as such is there to help him.

180   *prescience:* knowledge of the future; precognition

181   *zenith:* greatest happiness

183-184 *If now . . . droop:* If I don't take advantage of the present circumstances, I will never achieve my true destiny.

Master of this design, did give us, with
Rich garments, linens, stuffs and necessaries,
Which since have steaded much; so, of his gentleness, 165
Knowing I loved my books, he furnish'd me
From mine own library with volumes that
I prize above my dukedom.
Miranda: Would I might
But ever see that man!
Prospero: Now I arise:
                    [*Resumes his mantle.*]
Sit still, and hear the last of our sea-sorrow. 170
Here in this island we arrived; and here
Have I, thy schoolmaster, made thee more profit
Than other princesse can, that have more time
For vainer hours, and tutors not so careful.
Miranda: Heavens thank you for't! And now, I pray you,
        sir, 175
For still 'tis beating in my mind, your reason
For raising this sea-storm?
Prospero: Know thus far forth.
By accident most strange, bountiful Fortune,
Now my dear lady, hath mine enemies
Brought to this shore; and by my prescience 180
I find my zenith doth depend upon
A most auspicious star, whose influence
If now I court not, but omit, my fortunes
Will ever after droop. Here cease more questions:
Thou art inclined to sleep; 'tis a good dulness, 185
And give it way: I know thou canst not choose.
                    [*Miranda sleeps.*]
Come away, servant, come. I am ready now.
Approach, my Ariel, come.
[*Enter Ariel.*]
Ariel: All hail, great master! Grave, sir, hail! I come
To answer thy best pleasure; be't to fly, 190
To swim, to dive into the fire, to ride
On the curl'd clouds, to thy strong bidding task
Ariel and all his quality.
Prospero: Hast thou, spirit,
Perform'd to point the tempest that I bade thee?

29

196 *beak:* the front part of the ship

197 *waist:* the middle of the ship

198 *I flamed amazement:* Ariel appeared in the form of lightning flashes dashing here, there, and everywhere on the ship.

200 *yards:* long poles to which sails are attached; *bowsprit:* another kind of pole used to support rigging; *distinctly:* in separate parts

201 *precursors:* forerunners. Lightning always precedes the thunder clap.

203 *sight-outrunning:* The lightning flashes were so rapid that the eye could not trace their path.

207 *coil:* uproar

208-209 *Not a soul/ . . . mad:* Everyone felt as if they were going mad.

213 *hair up-staring:* hair standing on end

218 *sustaining garments:* Perhaps the garments kept the survivors afloat as they entered the waters.

223 *In an odd angle:* in a hidden corner

224 *in this sad knot:* Ariel describes Ferdinand's physical position as he sat in amazement upon the beach.

225 *how thou hast disposed:* what you did with

Ariel: To every article.   195
   I boarded the king's ship; now on the beak,
   Now in the waist, the deck, in every cabin,
   I flamed amazement: sometime I'd divide,
   And burn in many places; on the topmast,
   The yards and bowsprit, would I flame distinctly,   200
   Then meet and join. Jove's lightnings, the precursors
   O' the dreadful thunder-claps, more momentary
   And sight-outrunning were not: the fire and cracks
   Of sulphurous roaring the most mighty Neptune
   Seem to besiege, and make his bold waves tremble,   205
   Yea, his dread trident shake.
Prospero: My brave spirit!
   Who was so firm, so constant, that this coil
   Would not infect his reason?
Ariel: Not a soul
   But felt a fever of the mad, and play'd
   Some tricks of desperation. All but mariners   210
   Plunged in the foaming brine and quit the vessel,
   Then all afire with me: the king's son, Ferdinand,
   With hair up-staring,—then like reeds, not hair,—
   Was the first man that leap'd; cried, "Hell is empty,
   And all the devils are here."
Prospero: Why, that's my spirit!   215
   But was not this nigh shore?
Ariel: Close by, my master.
Prospero: But are they, Ariel, safe?
Ariel: Not a hair perish'd;
   On their sustaining garments not a blemish,
   But fresher than before: and, as thou badest me,
   In troops I have dispersed them 'bout the isle.   220
   The king's son have I landed by himself;
   Whom I left cooling of the air with sighs
   In an odd angle of the isle, and sitting,
   His arms in this sad knot.
Prospero: Of the king's ship,
   The mariners, say how thou hast disposed,   225
   And all the rest o' the fleet.
Ariel: Safely in harbour
   Is the king's ship; in the deep nook, where once

229   *still-vex'd Bermoothes:* The sea around Bermuda was reported by Elizabethan explorers to be very stormy. Bermoothes was the name applied to Bermuda in Shakespeare's time and although not geographically accurate as a stop on a voyage from Tunis to Naples it was a centre of interest to Elizabethan society in terms of the explorations of the New World that were occurring at the time this play was first presented.

230   *under hatches stow'd:* The sailors were placed in hatches (wooden coverings) below deck

231   *charm:* a song that lulled them into a form of dream-like sleep; *their suffer'd labour:* the work they had done in fighting against the storm

234   *flote:* waves of the sea

239   *mid season:* soon

240   *two glasses:* two o'clock in the afternoon. Time was measured by the hourglass.

241   *Must by . . . preciously:* There is not a minute to waste.

242   *give me pains:* employ me in difficult work

244   *How now? Moody?:* Are you in a bad mood?

250   *bate me:* reduce my time of service

252   *to tread the ooze:* to travel the muddy depths of the ocean

255   *the veins o' the earth:* the streams which ran underneath the earth's surface

256   *baked:* caked

Thou call'dst me up at midnight to fetch dew
From the still-vex'd Bermoothes, there she's hid:
The mariners all under hatches stow'd;   230
Who, with a charm join'd to their suffer'd labour,
I have left asleep; and for the rest o' the fleet,
Which I dispersed, they all have met again,
And are upon the Mediterranean flote,
Bound sadly home for Naples;   235
Supposing that they saw the king's ship wreck'd,
And his great person perish.

Prospero: Ariel, thy charge
Exactly is perform'd: but there's more work.
What is the time o' the day?

Ariel: Past the mid season.

Prospero: At least two glasses. The time 'twixt six and now 240
Must by us both be spent most preciously.

Ariel: Is there more toil? Since thou dost give me pains,
Let me remember thee what thou hast promised,
Which is not yet perform'd me.

Prospero: How now? Moody?
What is't thou canst demand?

Ariel: My liberty.   245

Prospero: Before the time be out? No more!

Ariel: I prithee,
Remember I have done thee worthy service;
Told thee no lies, made thee no mistakings, served
Without or grudge or grumblings: thou didst promise
To bate me a full year.

Prospero: Dost thou forget   250
From what a torment I did free thee?

Ariel: No.

Prospero: Thou dost; and think'st it much to tread the ooze
Of the salt deep,
To run upon the sharp wind of the north,
To do me business in the veins o' the earth   255
When it is baked with frost.

Ariel: I do not, sir.

Prospero: Thou liest, malignant thing! Hast thou forgot
The foul witch Sycorax, who with age and envy
Was grown into a hoop? hast thou forgot her?

261 *Argier:* Algiers, in the north of Africa

264 *manifold:* various, multiple

266 *for one thing she did:* for one good deed that she did

269 *blue-eyed hag:* An early stage of a woman's pregnancy was signified by a blue or dark circle appearing beneath her eyelid.

274 *hests:* commends, orders

275 *more potent ministers:* more powerful evil helpers

276 *unmitigable:* unforgiving. Sycorax was incapable of pity.

277 *rift:* position

280 *vent:* cry out

283 *whelp:* an offspring of a wild dog or wolf

288-289 *penetrate the . . . bears:* Even the savage bears felt pity for Ariel's sufferings imprisoned as he was in the pine tree.

292 *gape:* free, open

Ariel: No, sir.
Prospero:　　Thou hast. Where was she born? speak; tell
　　me.　　　　　　　　　　　　　　　　　　　　　　260
Ariel: Sir, in Argier.
Prospero:　　　　　O, was she so? I must
　　Once in a month recount what thou hast been,
　　Which thou forget'st. This damn'd witch Sycorax, → sik-or-ax.
　　For mischiefs manifold and sorceries terrible
　　To enter human hearing, from Argier,　　　　　265
　　Thou know'st, was banish'd: for one thing she did
　　They would not take her life. Is not this true?
Ariel: Ay, sir.
Prospero: This blue-eyed hag was hither brought with child,
　　And here was left by the sailors. Thou, my slave,　　270
　　As thou report'st thyself, wast then her servant;
　　And, for thou wast a spirit too delicate
　　To act her earthy and abhorr'd commands,
　　Refusing her grand hests, she did confine thee,
　　By help of her more potent ministers　　　　　275
　　And in her most unmitigable rage,
　　Into a cloven pine; within which rift
　　Imprison'd thou didst painfully remain
　　A dozen years; within which space she died,
　　And left thee there; where thou didst vent thy groans　280
　　As fast as mill-wheels strike. Then was this island—
　　Save for the son that she did litter here,
　　A freckled whelp hag-born—not honour'd with
　　A human shape.　　→ how the monster came to be.
Ariel:　　　　　Yes, Caliban her son.
Prospero: Dull thing, I say so; he, that Caliban,　　285
　　Whom now I keep in service. Thou best know'st
　　What torment I did find thee in; thy groans
　　Did make wolves howl, and penetrate the breasts
　　Of ever-angry bears: it was a torment
　　To lay upon the damn'd, which Sycorax　　　　290
　　Could not again undo: it was mine art,
　　When I arrived and heard thee, that made gape
　　The pine, and let thee out.
Ariel:　　　　　I thank thee, master.

294   *rend an oak:* tear open the trunk of an oak tree

297   *correspondent to command:* obedient to your commands

298   *do my spiriting gently:* gently and graciously carry out my
        services as a spirit

304   *go, hence with diligence:* Depart and carefully carry out my
        orders.

311   *We cannot miss him:* We could not manage without him.

314   *Thou earth, thou:* you foul, degraded creature

316   *When?:* an expression of impatience

317   *quaint:* neat, dainty, inventive

319-320 *got by . . . dam:* fathered by the devil himself as he lay upon
        your wicked mother, Sycorax

321-323 *As wicked . . . both:* People in Shakespeare's time believed
        in witches. The raven's wing was considered as a sign of
        bad luck and was believed to be used by witches in their
        sorceries. Caliban curses Prospero, wishing that poison-
        ous dew gathered by his mother with a raven's wing from a
        polluted marsh might drop upon him and his daughter.

Prospero: If thou more murmur'st, I will rend an oak,
   And peg thee in his knotty entrails, till   295
   Thou has howl'd away twelve winters.
Ariel: Pardon, master:
   I will be correspondent to command,
   And do my spiriting gently.
Prospero: Do so; and after two days
   I will discharge thee.
Ariel: That's my noble master!
   What shall I do? Say what; what shall I do?   300
Prospero: Go make thyself like a nymph o' the sea;
   Be subject to no sight but mine; invisible
   To every eyeball else. Go take this shape
   And hither come in't: go, hence with diligence!
                            [*Exit Ariel.*]
   Awake, dear heart, awake! Thou hast slept well;   305
   Awake!
Miranda: The strangeness of your story put
   Heaviness in me.
Prospero: Shake it off. Come on;
   We'll visit Caliban my slave, who never
   Yields us kind answer.
Miranda: 'Tis a villain, sir,
   I do not love to look on.
Prospero: But, as 'tis,   310
   We cannot miss him: he does make our fire,
   Fetch in our wood, and serves in offices
   That profit us. What, ho! Slave! Caliban!
   Thou earth, thou! Speak.
Caliban: [*Within*]   There's wood enough within.
Prospero: Come forth, I say! There's other business for thee: 315
    Come, thou tortoise! When?
   [*Re-enter Ariel like a water-nymph.*]
   Fine apparition! My quaint Ariel,
   Hark in thine ear.
Ariel: My lord, it shall be done.   [*Exit.*]
Prospero: Thou poisonous slave, got by the devil himself
   Upon thy wicked dam, come forth!   320
   [*Enter Caliban.*]
Caliban: As wicked dew as e'er my mother brush'd

323 *south-west:* The south-west wind was supposed to be very injurious; it was believed that this wind carried disease and pestilence.

326 *Side-stitches:* sudden and painful contractions in the side making breathing difficult; *pen:* close up

326-329 *urchins/Shall . . . honeycomb:* Prospero continues to punish Caliban by saying that "urchins" (evil goblins who at night travelled in the form of hedgehogs) will throughout the night pinch and otherwise torment ("exercise") him.

334 *Water with berries in't:* a beverage which Prosper gave him, perhaps the berries mentioned here refer to coffee beans

335-336 *the bigger . . . night:* a reference to the Book of Genesis: "God then made two great lights: the greater light to rule the day, and the less light to rule the night." *＊ Sun + moon.*

338 *brine-pits:* salt pits

345 *stripes:* lashes administered by a whip

350-351 *I had . . . isle:* I would have populated the island

352-353 *Which any . . . ill:* Caliban's nature is so corrupt that it is impossible to improve it.

356 *gabble:* jabber, brutish noises

357-358 *I endow'd . . . known:* Prospero taught Caliban language to give shape and meaning to his thoughts.

With raven's feather from unwholesome fen
Drop on you both! A south-west blow on ye
And blister you all o'er!
Prospero: For this, be sure, to-night thou shalt have cramps,   325
  Side-stitches that shall pen thy breath up; urchins
  Shall, for that vast of night that they may work,
  All exercise on thee; thou shalt be pinch'd
  As thick as honeycomb, each pinch more stinging
  Than bees that made 'em.
Caliban: I must eat my dinner.   330
  This island's mine, by Sycorax my mother,
  Which thou takest from me. When thou camest first,
  Thou strokedst me and madest much of me, wouldst give
    me
  Water with berries in't; and teach me how
  To name the bigger light, and how the less,   335
  That burn by day and night: and then I loved thee,
  And show'd thee all the qualities o' the isle,
  The fresh springs, brine-pits, barren place and fertile:
  Cursed be I that did so! All the charms
  Of Sycorax, toads, beetles, bats, light on you!   340
  For I am all the subjects that you have,
  Which first was mine own king: and here you sty me
  In this hard rock, whiles you do keep from me
  The rest o' the island.
Prospero: Thou most lying slave,
  Whom stripes may move, not kindness! I have used thee,   345
  Filth as thou art, with human care, and lodged thee
  In mine own cell, till thou didst seek to violate
  The honour of my child.
Caliban: O ho, O ho: would't had been done!
  Thou didst prevent me; I had peopled else   350
  This isle with Calibans.
Prospero: Abhorred slave,
  Which any print of goodness wilt not take,
  Being capable of all ill! I pitied thee,
  Took pains to make thee speak, taught thee each hour
  One thing or other: when thou didst not, savage,   355
  Know thine own meaning, but wouldst gabble like
  A thing most brutish, I endow'd thy purposes

362   *deserved more than a prison:* In Prospero's opinion Caliban deserved more severe punishment than imprisonment.

364   *red plague:* a reference to a plague caused red sores to appear on the body; *rid:* destroy

366   *thou'rt best:* It would be best for you.

369   *rack:* torture; *old clamps:* cramps such as old people would suffer

371   *din:* loud and disturbing noise

373   *Setebos:* a god worshipped by the Patagons in southern South America

374   *vassal:* a slave, bondsman

377-378 *kiss'd/The wild waves whist:* kissed the wild waves into silence

379   *Foot it featly:* dance nimbly

380   *the burthen bear:* Join with me in singing the chorus.

Stage direction – *[Burthen: Dispersedly.]:* The chorus of spirits sing randomly while Ariel is singing.

386   *chanticleer:* the male rooster (cock) who clearly sings out at dawn

With words that made them known. But thy vile race,
Though thou didst learn, had that in't which good natures
Could not abide to be with; therefore wast thou   360
Deservedly confined into this rock,
Who hadst deserved more than a prison.
Caliban: You taught me language; and my profit on't
  Is, I know how to curse. The red plague rid you
  For learning me your language!
Prospero: Hag-seed, hence!   365
  Fetch us in fuel; and be quick, thou'rt best,
  To answer other business. Shrug'st thou, malice?
  If thou neglect'st, or dost unwillingly
  What I command, I'll rack thee with old cramps,
  Fill all thy bones with aches, make thee roar,   370
  That beasts shall tremble at thy din.
Caliban: No, pray thee.
  [*Aside.*] I must obey: his art is of such power,
  It would control my dam's god, Setebos,
  And make a vassal of him.
Prospero: So, slave; hence!
                          [*Exit Caliban.*]
  [*Re-enter Ariel, invisible, playing and singing, Ferdinand
    following.*]
Ariel: *Come unto these yellow sands,*   375
      And then take hands:
    Courtsied when you have and kiss'd
      The wild waves whist:
    Foot it featly here and there;
    And, sweet sprites, the burthen bear.   380
      Hark, hark!
  [*Burthen: Dispersedly.*] *Bow-wow.*
Ariel: *The watch-dogs bark:*
  [*Burthen: Dispersedly.*] *Bow-wow.*
Ariel: *Hark, hark! I hear*   385
    The strain of strutting chanticleer
    Cry, Cock-a-diddle-dow.
Ferdinand: Where should this music be? I' the air or th'
  earth?
  It sounds no more: and, sure, it waits upon
  Some god o' th' island. Sitting on a bank,   390

Weeping again the king my father's wreck,
This music crept by me upon the waters,
Allaying both their fury and my passion
With its sweet air: thence I have follow'd it,
Or it hath drawn me rather. But 'tis gone.   395
No, it begins again.
Ariel:　*Full fathom five thy father lies;*
　　　　Of his bones are coral made;
　　　　Those are pearls that were his eyes:
　　　　Nothing of him that doth fade   400
　　　　But doth suffer a sea-change
　　　　Into something rich and strange.
　　　　Sea-nymphs hourly ring his knell:
　　　　　　Burthen: Ding-dong.
Ariel: Hark! Now I hear them,—*Ding-dong, bell.*
Ferdinand: The ditty does remember my drown'd father.   405
This is no mortal business, nor no sound
That the earth owes:—I hear it now above me.
Prospero: The fringed curtains of thine eye advance
And say what thou seest yond.
Miranda:　　　　　　　　　What is't? A spirit?
Lord, how it looks about! Believe me, sir,   410
It carries a brave form. But 'tis a spirit.
Prospero: No, wench; it eats and sleeps and hath such senses
As we have, such. This gallant which thou seest
Was in the wreck; and, but he's something stain'd
With grief, that's beauty's canker, thou mightst call him   415
A goodly person: he hath lost his fellows,
And strays about to find 'em.
Miranda:　　　　　　　　　I might call him
A thing divine; for nothing natural
I ever saw so noble.
Prospero: [*Aside.*]　　　It goes on, I see,
As my soul prompts it. Spirit, fine spirit! I'll free thee 420
Within two days for this.
Ferdinand:　　　　　　　Most sure, the goddess
On whom these airs attend! Vouchsafe my prayer
May know if you remain upon this island;
And that you will some good instruction give
How I may bear me here: my prime request,   425

428   *My language:* i.e., the language of Naples

429   *the best of them:* the highest ranking citizen of Naples. Assuming his father is now dead Ferdinand believes himself to be the king.

432   *A single thing:* myself and the King of Naples are now the same thing

435   *never since at ebb:* since the shipwreck my eyes have never stopped shedding tears

438-440 *The Duke . . . do't:* The real Duke of Milan and his daughter could disprove your statement if it were now the time for such an explanation of these events.

441   *They have changed eyes:* They have fallen in love already.

448   *your affection not gone forth:* You do not belong to anyone else.

449   *Soft, sir:* Gently, sir; be silent, sir.

451-452 *lest too . . . light:* Prospero plans to intervene in Ferdinand's wooing of Miranda since he fears that Ferdinand will value Miranda less if her love is too easily obtained.

454   *owest:* own

Which I do last pronounce, is, O you wonder!
If you be maid or no?
Miranda: No wonder, sir;
But certainly a maid.
Ferdinand: My language! Heavens!
I am the best of them that speak this speech,
Were I but where 'tis spoken.
Prospero: How? The best?   430
What wert thou, if the King of Naples heard thee?
Ferdinand: A single thing, as I am now, that wonders
To hear thee speak of Naples. He does hear me;
And that he does I weep: myself am Naples,
Who with mine eyes, never since at ebb, beheld   435
The king my father wreck'd.
Miranda: Alack, for mercy!
Ferdinand: Yes, faith, and all his lords; the Duke of Milan
And his brave son being twain.
Prospero: [*Aside.*]   The Duke of Milan
And his more braver daughter could control thee,
If now 'twere fit to do't. At the first sight   440
They have changed eyes. Delicate Ariel,
I'll set thee free for this. [*To Ferdinand.*] A word, good
    sir;
I fear you have done yourself some wrong: a word.
Miranda: Why speaks my father so ungently? This
Is the third man that e'er I saw; the first   445
That e'er I sigh'd for: pity move my father
To be inclined my way!
Ferdinand: O, if a virgin,
And your affection not gone forth, I'll make you
The Queen of Naples.
Prospero: Soft, sir! one word more.
[*Aside.*] They are both in either's powers; but this swift
    business   450
I must uneasy make, lest too light winning
Make the prize light. [*To Ferdinand.*] One word more; I
    charge thee
That thou attend me: thou dost here usurp
The name thou owest not; and hast put thyself

457   *temple:* body

467   *rash:* sudden, hasty

468   *fearful:* a person to fear

469   *My foot my tutor?:* Prospero chastizes Miranda for speaking up in defence of Ferdinand: Why should I listen to you, a child? I may as well let my foot become my teacher.

471   *come from thy ward:* Don't stand in that position of defence against me.

475   *I'll be his surety:* Miranda is so sure that Ferdinand is not an imposter that she pledges her very integrity as a guarantee of his honesty.

476   *chide:* chastise, scold

477   *An advocate for an impostor:* You speak on behalf of an imposter.

Upon this island as a spy, to win it   455
From me, the lord on't.
Ferdinand: No, as I am a man.
Miranda: There's nothing ill can dwell in such a temple:
   If the ill spirit have so fair a house,
   Good things will strive to dwell with't.
Prospero: Follow me.
   Speak not you for him; he's a traitor. Come;   460
   I'll manacle thy neck and feet together:
   Sea-water shalt thou drink; thy food shall be
   The fresh-brook muscles, wither'd roots, and husks
   Wherein the acorn cradled. Follow.
Ferdinand: No;
   I will resist such entertainment till   465
   Mine enemy has more power.
                     [*Draws and is charmed from moving.*]
Miranda: O dear father,
   Make not too rash a trial of him, for
   He's gentle and not fearful.
Prospero: What? I say,
   My foot my tutor? Put thy sword up, traitor;
   Who makest a show but darest not strike, thy conscience 470
   Is so possess'd with guilt: come from thy ward;
   For I can here disarm thee with this stick
   And make thy weapon drop.
Miranda: Beseech you, father.
Prospero: Hence! Hang not on my garments.
Miranda: Sir, have pity;
   I'll be his surety.
Prospero: Silence! One word more   475
   Shall make me chide thee, if not hate thee. What!
   An advocate for an impostor! Hush!
   Thou think'st there is no more such shapes as he,
   Having seen but him and Caliban: foolish wench!
   To the most of men this is a Caliban,   480
   And they to him are angels.
Miranda: My affections
   Are, then, most humble; I have no ambition
   To see a goodlier man.

484-485 *Thy nerves . . . them:* Your body is as an infant's; it is completely empty of energy.

486   *bound up:* incapable of physical movement

495   *Hark what . . . me:* Listen to what else I want you to do for me.

497   *this is unwonted:* this is unusual

Prospero: Come on; obey:
  Thy nerves are in their infancy again,
  And have no vigour in them.
Ferdinand: So they are: 485
  My spirits, as in a dream, are all bound up.
  My father's loss, the weakness which I feel,
  The wreck of all my friends, nor this man's threats,
  To whom I am subdued, are but light to me,
  Might I but through my prison once a day 490
  Behold this maid: all corners else o' the earth
  Let liberty make use of; space enough
  Have I in such a prison.
Prospero: [Aside.] It works.
        [*To Ferdinand.*] Come on.
  Thou hast done well, fine Ariel!
        [*To Ferdinand.*] Follow me.
  [*To Ariel.*] Hark what thou else shalt do me.
Miranda: Be of comfort: 495
    My father's of a better nature, sir,
  Than he appears by speech: this is unwonted
  Which now came from him.
Prospero: Thou shalt be as free
  As mountain winds: but then exactly do
  All points of my command.
Ariel: To the syllable. 500
Prospero: Come, follow. Speak not for him. [*Exeunt.*]

Ferdy shows up + goes ILYb!

49

Act 1, Scene 2: Activities

1. Because Prospero (an otherwise very intelligent man) did not seem to understand the responsibilities of being a duke, he lost his authority and dukedom. Write a letter to Prospero, explaining to him why you think he failed to hold power and rule successfully. Share your letter with classmates.

2. With a partner, choose one of the five characters introduced in this scene and role-play an interview with the character. Prepare a list of questions you will ask. The final question might be, "What do you think the future holds for you?" When you have completed the interview, reverse roles with your partner, and conduct the interview again.

   Write a newspaper article based on the interview. Introduce your article by explaining some of the background for your characters.

   As a class, create a chart on which you record ideas presented in the articles about the five characters. You might want to update the chart as the play progresses.

3. Costumes usually reveal to the audience visual details about the characters. They also help the audience understand relationships that exist between characters. With a group, consider the relationship that exists between Prospero and Miranda, or the one between Ariel and Caliban. Provide sketches or pictures of costumes for the two characters you have selected. Indicate the colours, fabrics, and ornamentation for each costume. Certain lines in the text may suggest images to support your ideas. Present the finished sketches to your classmates.

4. Reread Ariel's account of the tempest (lines 195–214). As a film director, use this information to create a

storyboard (a series of drawings that indicate the content, type, and sequence of camera shots that will be needed when filming) for the events during the tempest. How might you ensure that Ariel's role in the events which take place is clearly evident to the audience? Share your storyboard with classmates.

5. Examine the lyrics of the two songs that Ariel sings to Ferdinand (lines 375–387 and 397–404). If you were directing a modern version of this play, what music would you choose to accompany each song? As you consider the choices you would make, remember that you want to capture the mood and the message of each song.

   Share your ideas by playing segments of the music you have selected to your classmates.

6. In a group, discuss whether or not you think it's possible to fall in love at first sight. As Ferdinand or Miranda, write a diary entry describing and commenting on your first meeting with the other. You might include the circumstances and events which were part of the occasion. Share your entry with classmates.

7. If you were Caliban, how might you feel about the fact that Prospero has taken the rule of the island away from you? As Caliban write a diary entry revealing your thoughts about Prospero.

8. As Miranda, Ferdinand, Caliban, or Ariel, write a journal entry describing Prospero as you know and understand him at this point in the story. Share and compare your entries with classmates.

Act 1: Consider the Whole Act

1. Prospero obviously has a very detailed plan established for what he hopes to achieve in the next few hours. We now know something of his plan, although many of the details are not yet apparent. As Prospero, set up a plan of action in which you state your goals and list the steps you intend to follow to achieve them.

   Share your plan with classmates, noting similarities and differences in the steps you developed. As the play progresses refer to the plan you outlined and make any adjustments needed.

2. Recall the characters you have met to this point. If you were a casting director, what modern actors would you select for each role? Give reasons for your choices, mentioning details such as the actor's performing abilities, appearance, and other roles he/she has played that would support this role. Share your list with others and reach a consensus about the most effective cast of characters.

3. With a partner, create a children's fairy tale, using Act 1 to develop the story outline. You might begin with, "Once upon a time, there was a beautiful princess named Miranda." Organize the details of your story so they can be understood easily by readers. Keep your story line short and uncomplicated. Include illustrations to support your story text.

   Add to your story as you continue reading the play. When you have completed your fairy tale, present it to students in an elementary school class.

4. As Ferdinand, write a speech in modern or Shakespearean English in which you tell Miranda about what happened on board ship and how you felt during the storm. Where might you insert your speech in this act?

Read your speech to classmates, and have them assess how effectively it reveals the information you wanted to communicate.

5. Dramatize the story of Prospero's past, Scene 2, lines 53–168, by selecting a story-teller (Prospero) and several other class members to portray the characters in his tale. The story-teller may move among the actors while telling the story, but the actors must pay no attention to the story-teller. The actors may perform their lines by reading them only, by using actions only (mime) or by combining the two. Present your production to the class.

For the next scene . . .

Think of political events of the twentieth century which involved evil persons attempting to take over or hold onto leadership of a government. Did they succeed in their efforts? If not, why and how were they stopped? Discuss your ideas and/or write your thoughts in a journal entry.

Act 2, Scene 1

In this scene . . .

The royal passengers on board the ship having
escaped drowning, are wandering about the island.
Alonso, King of Naples, is suffering because he
believes his son Ferdinand has drowned. Although
Adrian and Gonzalo try to console him, Antonio and
Sebastian show no sympathy.

After Ariel has put everyone to sleep except for
Antonio and Sebastian, Antonio persuades Sebastian
to seize this opportunity to kill his brother Alonso and
become King of Naples. As Sebastian kills Alonso,
they agree that Antonio will murder Gonzalo. Their
plans, however, are thwarted by Ariel's intervention.
Gonzalo suddenly awakens to discover Antonio and
Sebastian with their swords drawn to attack. Sebastian
explains their actions by claiming they pulled out their
swords when they heard the roaring of lions. Afraid
of being attacked, the royal party leaves to continue
their search for Ferdinand.

3-4   *Our hint . . . common:* Our cause of sorrow (i.e. the shipwreck) is a common occurrence.

5   *merchant, and the merchant:* the trading ship and the owner of the vessel

8-9   *weigh/Our . . . comfort:* Think not only of our grief but also of the comforting fact that we have escaped death.

10   *like cold porridge:* cold porridge is not a welcome or gratifying meal

11   *The visitor . . . o'er so:* Gonzalo is speaking like a visitor who has come to console the afflicted; he will not give up his attempts to try and make Alonso look at the bright side of their situation.

16   *entertain'd:* received

19   *Dolour:* sorrow, is a pun on "dollar," line 18

21   *taken it wiselier:* understood my pun

25   *spare:* space your words

Act 2, Scene 1

Another part of the island.

Enter Alonso, Sebastian, Antonio,
Gonzalo, Adrian, Francisco, and
others.

Gonzalo: Beseech you, sir, be merry; you have cause,
  So have we all, of joy; for our escape
  Is much beyond our loss. Our hint of woe
  Is common; every day, some sailor's wife,
  The masters of some merchant, and the merchant,   5
  Have just our theme of woe; but for the miracle,
  I mean our preservation, few in millions
  Can speak like us: then wisely, good sir, weigh
  Our sorrow with our comfort.
Alonso: Prithee, peace.
Sebastian: He receives comfort like cold porridge.   10
Antonio: The visitor will not give him o'er so.
Sebastian: Look, he's winding up the watch of his wit; by
    and by it will strike.
Gonzalo: Sir,—
Sebastian: One: tell.   15
Gonzalo: When every grief is entertain'd that's offer'd,
  Comes to the entertainer—
Sebastian: A dollar.
Gonzalo: Dolour comes to him, indeed: you have spoken
    truer than you purposed.   20
Sebastian: You have taken it wiselier than I meant you
    should.
Gonzalo: Therefore, my lord,—
Antonio: Fie, what a spendthrift is he of his tongue!
Alonso: I prithee, spare.   25

28-29 *Which, of . . . crow?:* Let's wager which of Gonzalo or Adrian will speak first.

30 *The old cock:* Gonzalo

31 *The cockerel:* Adrian

34 *A match:* It's a bet.

42 *temperance:* temperature, which is used in line 43 as a girl's name

49 *save:* except

51 *lush and lusty:* strong and rich

53 *eye:* tinge

58 *vouched rarities:* things guaranteed by their owners to be rare

65 *pocket up his report:* accept what he says to be true

Gonzalo: Well, I have done: but yet,—
Sebastian: He will be talking.
Antonio: Which, of he or Adrian, for a good wager, first
    begins to crow?
Sebastian: The old cock.   30
Antonio: The cockerel.
Sebastian: Done. The wager?
Antonio: A laughter.
Sebastian: A match!
Adrian: Though this island seem to be desert,—   35
Sebastian: Ha, ha, ha!—So, you're paid.
Adrian: Uninhabitable and almost inaccessible,—
Sebastian: Yet,—
Adrian: Yet,—
Antonio: He could not miss't.   40
Adrian: It must needs be of subtle, tender and delicate
    temperance.
Antonio: Temperance was a delicate wench.
Sebastian: Ay, and a subtle: as he most learnedly delivered.
Adrian: The air breathes upon us here most sweetly.   45
Sebastian: As if it had lungs and rotten ones.
Antonio: Or as 'twere perfumed by a fen.
Gonzalo: Here is everything advantageous to life.
Antonio: True: save means to live.
Sebastian: Of that there's none, or little.   50
Gonzalo: How lush and lusty the grass looks! how green!
Antonio: The ground, indeed, is tawny.
Sebastian: With an eye of green in't.
Antonio: He misses not much.
Sebastian: No; he doth but mistake the truth totally.   55
Gonzalo: But the rarity of it is,—which is indeed almost
    beyond credit,—
Sebastian: As many vouched rarities are.
Gonzalo: That our garments, being, as they were, drenched
    in the sea, hold, notwithstanding, their freshness and   60
    glosses, being rather new-dyed than stained with salt
    water.
Antonio: If but one of his pockets could speak, would it
    not say he lies?
Sebastian: Ay, or very falsely pocket up his report.   65

71   *paragon:* ideal match

73   *widow Dido's time:* This is a reference to Queen Dido the
        founder and first queen of Carthage, near Tunis. Although
        she was a widow when she met and fell in love with Aeneas,
        the various stories of their love for each other never
        acknowledge her as having been widowed by an earlier hus-
        band. Gonzalo's reference to Dido as a widow would have
        been a source of humour to Shakespeare's audiences as it is
        to Antonio and Sebastian.

77   *how you take it:* How you laugh at it! Sebastian is enjoying
        Antonio's responses to Gonzalo's reference to Dido, the
        widow.

83   *the miraculous harp:* Amphion, the king of Thebes, played the
        harp with such magical skill that he was able to charm the
        stones of the city to form themselves into a protecting wall.

84   *He hath . . . too:* In Gonzalo's mistaking Tunis for Carthage,
        Sebastian mocks Gonzalo as being even more talented
        than the king of Thebes.

96   *Bate:* omit; leave out

98   *doublet:* a lined jacket

99   *in a sort:* after a fashion; in a certain way

103   *The stomach of my sense:* I cannot stomach your feeble
        attempts to cheer me up.

105   *in my rate:* in my opinion

Gonzalo: Methinks our garments are now as fresh as when
    we put them on first in Afric, at the marriage of the
    king's fair daughter Claribel to the King of Tunis.

Sebastian: 'Twas a sweet marriage, and we prosper well in
    our return.   70

Adrian: Tunis was never graced before with such a paragon
    to their queen.

Gonzalo: Not since widow Dido's time.

Antonio: Widow! A pox o' that! How came that widow in?
    Widow Dido!   75

Sebastian: What if he had said "widower Æneas" too? Good
    Lord, how you take it!

Adrian: "Widow Dido" said you? You make me study of
    that: she was of Carthage, not of Tunis.

Gonzalo: This Tunis, sir, was Carthage.   80

Adrian: Carthage?

Gonzalo: I assure you, Carthage.

Antonio: His word is more than the miraculous harp.

Sebastian: He hath raised the wall and houses too.

Antonio: What impossible matter will he make easy next?   85

Sebastian: I think he will carry this island home in his
    pocket, and give it his son for an apple.

Antonio: And, sowing the kernels of it in the sea, bring forth
    more islands.

Gonzalo: Ay.   90

Antonio: Why, in good time.

Gonzalo: Sir, we were talking that our garments seem now
    as fresh as when we were at Tunis at the marriage
    of your daughter, who is now queen.

Antonio: And the rarest that e'er came there.   95

Sebastian: Bate, I beseech you, widow Dido.

Antonio: O, widow Dido! Ay, widow Dido.

Gonzalo: Is not, sir, my doublet as fresh as the first day I
    wore it? I mean, in a sort.

Antonio: That sort was well fished for.   100

Gonzalo: When I wore it at your daughter's marriage?

Antonio: You cram these words into mine ears against
    The stomach of my sense. Would I had never
    Married my daughter there! For, coming thence,
    My son is lost, and, in my rate, she too,   105

110   *the surges:* the waves

111-112 *he trod . . . aside:* He made his way against the waves which threatened to defeat him.

113   *The surge most swoln:* the largest waves

114   *contentious:* warring, opposing

116   *the shore . . . bow'd:* the shore seemed to bow in welcome

124   *importuned:* urgently asked; begged

127   *Which end . . . bow:* Claribel (Alonso's daughter, see line 68) did not know whether she should give in to her father's orders to marry the African prince or to her own feelings of loathing ("loathness") for the person she was being forced to marry.

129   *Mo:* more

131   *dear'st o' the loss:* Ferdinand, the most serious loss experienced in this whole affair

134   *And time . . . in:* a suitable time in which to speak of these errors in judgement of which Alonso is now his own victim

135   *plaster:* the bandage

136   *chirurgeonly:* like a surgeon

Who is so far from Italy removed
I ne'er again shall see her. O thou mine heir
Of Naples and of Milan, what strange fish
Hath made his meal on thee?
Francisco: Sir, he may live:
I saw him beat the surges under him,   110
And ride upon their backs; he trod the water,
Whose enmity he flung aside, and breasted
The surge most swoln that met him: his bold head
'Bove the contentious waves he kept, and oar'd
Himself with his good arms in lusty stroke   115
To the shore, that o'er his wave-worn basis bow'd
As stooping to relieve him: I not doubt
He came alive to land.
Alonso: No, no, he's gone.
Sebastian: Sir, you may thank yourself for this great loss,
That would not bless our Europe with your daughter,   120
But rather lose her to an African;
Where she at least is banish'd from your eye,
Who hath cause to wet the grief on't.
Alonso: Prithee, peace.
Sebastian: You were kneel'd to and importuned otherwise,
By all of us; and the fair soul herself   125
Weigh'd between loathness and obedience, at
Which end o' the beam should bow. We have lost your
   son,
I fear, for ever: Milan and Naples have
Mo widows in them of this business' making
Than we bring men to comfort them: 130
The fault's your own.
Alonso: So is the dear'st o' the loss.
Gonzalo: My lord Sebastian,
The truth you speak doth lack some gentleness,
And time to speak it in: you rub the sore,
When you should bring the plaster.
Sebastian: Very well.   135
Antonio: And most chirurgeonly.
Gonzalo: It is foul weather in us all, good sir,
When you are cloudy.

139 *Had I . . . isle:* were I in charge of setting up a colony on this island

140 *nettle-seed/Or docks, or mallows:* weeds

144 *traffic:* trade

146 *Letters:* academic learning

147 *use of service:* no servants would be allowed; *contract:* legal contracts; *succession:* legal inheritance of estates

148 *Bourn:* the boundary line of a piece of land; *bound of land:* a fixed plot of land enclosed within a boundary; *tilth:* tilled land; cultivation

155 *All things in common nature:* All natural resources would be available to anyone who has need of them.

156-157 *treason, felony/ . . . engine:* crimes and weapons

159 *foison:* plenty, rich harvests

164 *golden age:* that imaginary time in human history when all things were perfect

168 *minister occasion:* to take advantage of the opportunity

168-170 *of such/ . . . nothing:* To Gonzalo it seems that Antonio and Sebastian are the type of people who laugh at anything, even when they are in a serious situation.

Sebastian: Foul weather?
Antonio: Very foul.
Gonzalo: Had I plantation of this isle, my lord,—
Antonio: He'd sow't with nettle-seed.
Sebastian: Or docks, or mallows.   140
Gonzalo: And were the king on't, what would I do?
Sebastian: 'Scape being drunk for want of wine.
Gonzalo: I' the commonwealth I would by contraries
    Execute all things: for no kind of traffic
    Would I admit; no name of magistrate;   145
    Letters should not be known; riches, poverty,
    And use of service, none; contract, succession,
    Bourn, bound of land, tilth, vineyard, none;
    No use of metal, corn, or wine, or oil;
    No occupation: all men idle, all;   150
    And women too, but innocent and pure;
    No sovereignty;—
Sebastian: Yet he would be king on't.
Antonio: The latter end of his commonwealth forgets the
    beginning.
Gonzalo: All things in common nature should produce   155
    Without sweat or endeavour: treason, felony,
    Sword, pike, knife, gun, or need of any engine,
    Would I not have; but nature should bring forth,
    Of its own kind, all foison, all abundance,
    To feed my innocent people.   160
Sebastian: No marrying 'mong his subjects?
Antonio: None, man; all idle; whores and knaves.
Gonzalo: I would with such perfection govern, sir,
    To excel the golden age.
Sebastian: 'Save his majesty!
Antonio: Long live Gonzalo!
Gonzalo: And,—do you mark me, sir?   165
Alonso: Prithee, no more: thou dost talk nothing to me.
Gonzalo: I do well believe your highness; and did it to
    minister occasion to these gentlemen, who are of such
    sensible and nimble lungs that they always use to
    laugh at nothing.   170
Antonio: 'Twas you we laughed at.

175   *flat-long:* on the flat side (rather than the sharp edge) of a sword

176   *brave mettle:* courageous spirit

176-178 *you would/ . . . changing:* Yes, you are indeed brave men who would even attempt to do the impossible. Gonzalo is being very sarcastic.

179   *a bat-fowling:* to catch bats

181   *warrant:* promise

181-182 *adventure my dis-/cretion so weakly:* I would never risk my good sense or wisdom for such trivial matters as your mocking laughter.

185-186 *I wish . . . thoughts:* would, when they close in sleep, relieve me of these sad thoughts and feelings I am presently experiencing.

188   *omit the . . . it:* In other words, allow yourself to fall asleep and escape your worry and sorrow for a little while.

192   *Wondrous heavy:* It is strange that I should be so very sleepy.

196   *my spirits are nimble:* I am wide awake and full of energy.

199   *No more:* I do not dare to say more.

201   *the occasion speaks thee:* The circumstances in which we now find ourselves encourages you to take advantage of them and act quickly.

Gonzalo: Who in this kind of merry fooling am nothing to
    you: so you may continue, and laugh at nothing still.

Antonio: What a blow was there given!

Sebastian: And it had not fallen flat-long.   175

Gonzalo: You are gentlemen of brave mettle; you would
    lift the moon out of her sphere, if she would continue
    in it five weeks without changing.

    [*Entel Ariel, invisible, playing solemn music.*]

Sebastian: We would so, and then go a bat-fowling.

Antonio: Nay, good my lord, be not angry.   180

Gonzalo: No, I warrant you; I will not adventure my dis-
    cretion so weakly. Will you laugh me asleep, for I am
    very heavy?

Antonio: Go sleep, and hear us.

    [*All sleep except Alonso, Sebastian, and Antonio.*]

Alonso: What, all so soon asleep! I wish mine eyes   185
    Would, with themselves, shut up my thoughts: I find
    They are inclined to do so.

Sebastian: Please you, sir,
    Do not omit the heavy offer of it:
    It seldom visits sorrow; when it doth,
    It is a comforter.

Antonio: We two, my lord,   190
    Will guard your person while you take your rest,
    And watch your safety.

Alonso: Thank you.—Wondrous heavy.
              [*Alonso sleeps. Exit Ariel.*]

Sebastian: What a strange drowsiness possesses them!

Antonio: It is the quality o' the climate.

Sebastian: Why
    Doth it not then our eyelids sink? I find not   195
    Myself disposed to sleep.

Antonio: Nor I; my spirits are nimble.
    They fell together all, as by consent;
    They dropp'd, as by a thunder-stroke. What might,
    Worthy Sebastian?—O, what might?—No more:—
    And yet methinks I see it in thy face,   200
    What thou shouldst be: the occasion speaks thee; and
    My strong imagination sees a crown
    Dropping upon thy head.

205   *sleepy language:* You are speaking strangely and of danger-
        ous things as if you were speaking a dream.

210-211 *Thou let'st . . . waking:* You're letting an opportunity to become
        a greater person sleep or even perish; you're not seeing
        the chance you have before you.

215   *Trebles thee o'er:* makes you three times greater that you
        already are; *standing water:* I haven't decided which
        course of action to take

216-217 *to ebb/ . . . me:* my inclination is to back off and not to move
        for my own advancement; rather in idleness I would allow
        my fortunes to decline

218-222 *If you but . . . sloth:* Antonio uses Sebastian's metaphor of
        the ebbing sea to encourage him to take advantage of the
        situation. He warns Sebastian that men whose fortunes decline
        or who remain in a lowly position have only their own fear
        or laziness to blame.

223-225 *The setting . . . yield:* The look which I see in your eyes and
        upon your face show that you have an important idea that
        can only be acted upon with difficulty and pain.

226-230 *Although this . . . to persuade:* Antonio is referring to Gonzalo.
        He says that Gonzalo is a man with a failing memory (remem-
        bering the confusion he displayed when talking of Tunis
        and Carthage) who will not be remembered after he dies
        and who only speaks to persuade others of things which he
        does not fully believe himself.

Sebastian: What, art thou waking?
Antonio: Do you not hear me speak?
Sebastian: I do; and surely
  It is a sleepy language, and thou speak'st   205
  Out of thy sleep. What is it thou didst say?
  This is a strange repose, to be asleep
  With eyes wide open; standing, speaking, moving,
  And yet so fast asleep.
Antonio: Noble Sebastian,
  Thou let'st thy fortune sleep—die, rather; wink'st   210
  Whiles thou art waking.
Sebastian: Thou dost snore distinctly;
  There's meaning in thy snores.
Antonio: I am more serious than my custom: you
  Must be so too, if heed me; which to do
  Trebles thee o'er.
Sebastian: Well, I am standing water.   215
Antonio: I'll teach you how to flow.
Sebastian: Do so: to ebb
  Hereditary sloth instructs me.
Antonio: O,
  If you but knew how you the purpose cherish
  Whiles thus you mock it! How, in stripping it,
  You more invest it! Ebbing men, indeed,   220
  Most often do so near the bottom run
  By their own fear or sloth.
Sebastian: Prithee, say on:
  The setting of thine eye and cheek proclaim
  A matter from thee; and a birth, indeed,
  Which throes thee much to yield.
Antonio: Thus, sir: 225
  Although this lord of weak remembrance, this,
  Who shall be of as little memory
  When he is earth'd, hath here almost persuaded—
  For he's a spirit of persuasion, only
  Professes to persuade,—the king his son's alive,   230
  'Tis as impossible that he's undrown'd
  As he that sleeps here swims.
Sebastian: I have no hope
  That he's undrown'd.

236   *Ambition cannot . . . beyond:* There is no greater ambition than that to be the King of Naples.

237   *But doubt discovery there:* Once ambition has fulfilled itself in being the King of Naples it would never strive for anything greater.

241   *Ten leagues beyond man's life:* an exaggeration of the distance between Tunis and Naples

242-243   *post – /The . . . slow:* messenger, deliverer ("post"); the moon would take even longer to deliver the message than the sun

243   *new-born chins:* infants

245   *cast again:* were cast upon shore

246-248   *to perform . . . discharge:* to perform an act which recent events have prepared the way for, and that is now our responsibility to carry out

251   *cubit:* a unit of measurement – 18 inches

253   *Measure us back:* follow us; *Keep:* let her remain

254   *Say, this were death:* Let us imagine that these sleeping persons were dead.

256   *There be:* there is a person

259-260   *I myself . . . chat:* Antonio says that he could teach a bird to talk as meaningfully as Gonzalo speaks

260   *chough:* a crow-like bird; a type of jay

263-264   *And how . . . fortune?:* How do you intend to act under such fortunate circumstances as these in which you now find yourself?

Antonio: O, out of that "no hope"
What great hope have you! No hope that way is
Another way so high a hope that even   235
Ambition cannot pierce a wink beyond,
But doubt discovery there. Will you grant with me
That Ferdinand is drown'd?
Sebastian: He's gone.
Antonio: Then, tell me
Who's the next heir of Naples?
Sebastian: Claribel.
Antonio: She that is queen of Tunis; she that dwells   240
Ten leagues beyond man's life; she that from Naples
Can have no note, unless the sun were post—
The man i' the moon's too slow—till new-born chins
Be rough and razorable; she that from whom
We all were sea-swallow'd, though some cast again,   245
And by that destiny, to perform an act
Whereof what's past is prologue; what to come,
In yours and my discharge.
Sebastian: What stuff is this! How say
    you?
'Tis true, my brother's daughter's queen of Tunis;
So is she heir of Naples; 'twixt which regions   250
There is some space.
Antonio: A space whose every cubit
Seems to cry out, "How shall that Claribel
Measure us back to Naples? Keep in Tunis,
And let Sebastian wake." Say, this were death
That now hath seized them; why, they were no worse   255
Than now they are. There be that can rule Naples,
As well as he that sleeps; lords that can prate
As amply and unnecessarily
As this Gonzalo; I myself could make
A chough of as deep chat. O, that you bore   260
The mind that I do! What a sleep were this
For your advancement! Do you understand me?
Sebastian: Methinks I do.
Antonio: And how does your content
    Tender your own good fortune?

267   *feater:* more handsomely, more trimly

268   *fellows:* equals

269   *But, for your conscience:* except for your conscience. Sebastian wonders if Antonio's conscience must still bother him.

270   *kibe:* a inflammation and itchy skin irritation usually found on the feet or hands, chilblain

271   *'Twould put . . . slipper:* Antonio explains that the guilt he feels is no more troublesome than if it were a sore on his heel that would simply require him to wear a slipper in place of a shoe.

273   *candied:* crystalized sugar

273-274 *candied be . . . molest:* If I had twenty consciences, they would not keep me from getting what I wanted.

279   *perpetual wink for aye:* put Alonso to sleep forever

281   *Should not upbraid our course:* would not be able to scold us or censure our actions

283-284 *They'll tell . . . hour:* They'll do and say whatever we wish.

285   *precedent:* example

Sebastian: I remember
  You did supplant your brother Prospero.
Antonio: True: 265
  And look how well my garments sit upon me;
  Much feater than before: my brother's servants
  Were then my fellows: now they are my men.
Sebastian: But, for your conscience.
Antonio: Ay, sir; where lies that? If 'twere a kibe,   270
  'Twould put me to my slipper: but I feel not
  This deity in my bosom: twenty consciences,
  That stand 'twixt me and Milan, candied be they
  And melt, ere they molest! Here lies your brother,
  No better than the earth he lies upon,   275
  If he were that which now he's like, that's dead;
  Whom I, with this obedient steel, three inches of it,
  Can lay to bed for ever; whiles you, doing thus,
  To the perpetual wink for aye might put
  This ancient morsel, this Sir Prudence, who   280
  Should not upbraid our course. For all the rest,
  They'll take suggestion as a cat laps milk;
  They'll tell the clock to any business that
  We say befits the hour.
Sebastian: Thy case, dear friend,
  Shall be my precedent; as thou got'st Milan,   285
  I'll come by Naples. Draw thy sword: one stroke
  Shall free thee from the tribute which thou payest;
  And I the king shall love thee.
Antonio: Draw together;
  And when I rear my hand, do you the like,
  To fall it on Gonzalo.
Sebastian: O, but one word.   290
                    [They talk apart.]

[Re-enter Ariel, invisible.]
Ariel: My master through his art foresees the danger
  That you, his friend, are in; and sends me forth,—
  For else his project dies,—to keep them living.
                 [Sings in Gonzalo's ear.]

    While you here do snoring lie,   295
    Open-eyed conspiracy
    His time doth take.

315   *That's verily:* That is the truth.

> *If of life you keep a care,*
> *Shake off slumber and beware:*
> *Awake, awake!*

Antonio: Then let us both be sudden.
Gonzalo: Now, good angels   300
   Preserve the king!   [*They wake.*]
Alonso: Why, how now? ho, awake!—why are you drawn?
   Wherefore this ghastly looking?
Gonzalo: What's the matter?
Sebastian: Whiles we stood here securing your repose,
   Even now, we heard a hollow burst of bellowing   305
   Like bulls, or rather lions: did't not wake you?
   It struck mine ear most terribly.
Alonso: I heard nothing.
Antonio: O, 'twas a din to fright a monster's ear,
   To make an earthquake! sure, it was the roar
   Of a whole herd of lions.
Alonso: Heard you this, Gonzalo?   310
Gonzalo: Upon my honour, sir, I heard a humming,
   And that a strange one too, which did awake me:
   I shaked you, sir, and cried; as mine eyes open'd,
   I saw their weapons drawn:—there was a noise,
   That's verily. 'Tis best we stand upon our guard,   315
   Or that we quit this place: let's draw our weapons.
Alonso: Lead off this ground; and let's make further search
   For my poor son.
Gonzalo: Heavens keep him from these beasts!
   For he is, sure, i' the island.
Alonso: Lead away.
Ariel: Prospero my lord shall know what I have done   320
   So, king, go safely on to seek thy son.   [*Exeunt.*]

Act 2, Scene 1: Activities

1. At the beginning of the scene, Gonzalo and Adrian try to comfort Alonso about the loss of his son Ferdinand. Why do you think they fail to make him feel better? What would you have said differently if you had encountered Alonso at this time? Write a note or piece of prose to convey your feelings.

2. In a group consider how each of the characters in this scene responds to being on the island, using headings such as Positive/Negative or Optimistic/Pessimistic. If these characters had to live on the island for the next three years without Prospero, what do you think would happen to them? Imagine that you, as an archaeologist, visit the island years after the arrival of the characters. What do you think you would find?

3. In the first half of the scene, there are two separate (but linked) conversations happening at the same time. As Gonzalo and Adrian talk with each other, Antonio and Sebastian make sarcastic responses to what they hear. Which word play and/or puns that Antonio and Sebastian aim at Gonzalo do you find most effective?

   Imagine that you are directing the actors for these conversations. What recommendations would you make to both pairs of speakers about the way they should deliver their lines? Remember that the audience must be able to hear both conversations clearly. Discuss and try out your ideas with some classmates. You may wish to present this scene segment to the rest of the class.

4. Reread Gonzalo's description of his ideal state in his "Commonwealth" speech, lines 143–152. In a journal entry, record your sense of what he is saying, and his philosophy.

Imagine you are a newspaper reporter visiting Gonzalo's commonwealth. Write an article for the newspaper in which you provide details about the following:

a) what Gonzalo wants to have in his commonwealth,

b) what Gonzalo does not want.

5. In your journals complete, and if you wish expand upon, one or all of the following statements. Share and discuss your entries with classmates.
   • The character in this scene who represents most the kind of person in political society I fear is . . . because . . . .
   • Gonzalo reminds me of the type of person who . . . .
   • As I experienced this scene I was (or was not) aware of Prospero's influence because . . . .
   • The role I would enjoy playing most in this scene would be . . . because . . . .

For the next scene . . .

Recall movies, books, and television programs that you have found humorous. What elements, if any, did they have in common that made them funny? Do people you know respond to jokes and other forms of humour in the same way as you? What might account for similarities and/or differences in what people think is amusing? Discuss your ideas.

Act 2, Scene 2

In this scene . . .

Caliban wanders about the island still cursing Prospero and blaming him for all the hardship he suffers. Then he sees Trinculo, a jester from the shipwrecked royal party. Believing Trinculo to be one of Prospero's spirits, Caliban throws himself on the ground, hoping to escape notice. Trinculo, however, spots Caliban and considers how much he might make if he could take this bizarre creature home to Naples.

When Trinculo hears thunder, he takes refuge under Caliban's clothes. At this point, the drunken butler Stephano enters, having drifted ashore from the shipwreck by clinging to a barrel of wine. He investigates what looks to him like a four-legged creature with two mouths. After a comical exchange, Stephano pulls Trinculo out from under Caliban's cloak and the two are happily reunited. Caliban, now heavily under the influence of alcohol fed to him by Stephano, makes a vow to abandon Prospero and take Stephano as his master. As his first official service, Caliban drunkenly leads the pair (who are in the same condition) to show them the wonders of the island and secure some food for them.

3   *inch-meal:* by inches at a time, by slow degrees

5   *urchin-shows:* appearances or apparitions of small demons

6   *like a firebrand:* luminous gases given off by the swamps or marshes. It was believed that these lights were deliberately contrived by evil spirits – will-o'-the-wisp or jack-o'-lantern – to mislead a traveller from his destination.

9   *mow:* make faces

17   *mind me:* notice me

21   *bombard:* a wine container made of leather, which eventually would wear out and be likely to burst

27   *poor-John:* a coarse salt fish with an unpleasant odour

28   *painted:* as on a poster

Scene 2

Another part of the island.

*Enter Caliban with a burden of
wood. A noise of thunder heard.*

Caliban: All the infections that the sun sucks up
  From bogs, fens, flats, on Prosper fall, and make him
  By inch-meal a disease! His spirits hear me,
  And yet I needs must curse. But they'll nor pinch,
  Fright me with urchin-shows, pitch me i' the mire,   5
  Nor lead me, like a firebrand, in the dark
  Out of my way, unless he bid 'em; but
  For every trifle are they set upon me;
  Sometime like apes, that mow and chatter at me,
  And after bite me; then like hedgehogs, which   10
  Lie tumbling in my barefoot way, and mount
  Their pricks at my footfall; sometime am I
  All wound with adders, who with cloven tongues
  Do hiss me into madness.
  [*Enter Trinculo.*]
                          Lo, now, lo!
  Here comes a spirit of his, and to torment me   15
  For bringing wood in slowly. I'll fall flat;
  Perchance he will not mind me.
Trinculo: Here's neither bush nor shrub, to bear off any
  weather at all, and another storm brewing; I hear it sing
  i' the wind; yond same black cloud, yond huge one,   20
  looks like a foul bombard that would shed his liquor.
  If it should thunder as it did before, I know not
  where to hide my head: yond same cloud cannot choose
  but fall by pailfuls. What have we here? A man or a
  fish? Dead or alive? A fish: he smells like a fish; a   25
  very ancient and fish-like smell; a kind of, not of the
  newest, poor-John. A strange fish! Were I in England
  now, as once I was, and had but this fish painted, not
  a holiday fool there but would give a piece of silver:

30   *make a man:* i.e., make a man rich

31   *doit:* cain

33   *dead Indian:* Many natives of the new world were brought to England as trophies of the explorers' adventures. The natives were exhibited and became a source of profitable investment; most did not survive very long.

34   *let loose my opinion:* change my mind or opinion

38   *gaberdine:* a long smock worn as an outer garment

40   *shroud:* cover myself

43   *scurvy tune:* a miserable or vile song

45   *the swabber:* a sailor whose job is to wash the decks of the ship

49   *a tongue with a tang:* a person who usually utters sarcastic and sour-tempered speech

57   *Ind:* India

59-60 *As proper . . . ground:* This may be a modification of the popular proverb of the time which began with, "As proper a man as ever went on two legs."

65   *an ague:* a fever which causes the sufferer to shiver

there would this monster make a man: any strange beast 30
there makes a man: when they will not give a doit to
relieve a lame beggar, they will lay out ten to see a
dead Indian. Legged like a man! and his fins like arms!
Warm, o' my troth! I do now let loose my opinion;
hold it no longer: this is no fish, but an islander, that 35
hath lately suffered by a thunderbolt. [*Thunder.*] Alas,
the storm is come again! My best way is to creep under
his gaberdine; there is no other shelter hereabout:
misery acquaints a man with strange bed-fellows. I will
here shroud till the dregs of the storm be past. 40

[*Enter Stephano, singing: a bottle in his hand.*]

Stephano: *I shall no more to sea, to sea,*
           Here shall I die ashore,—
This is a very scurvy tune to sing at a man's
funeral: well, here's my comfort.   [*Drinks.*]
[*Sings.*]
    The master, the swabber, the boatswain and I, 45
      The gunner, and his mate,
  Loved Mall, Meg, and Marian, and Margery,
      But none of us cared for Kate;
    For she had a tongue with a tang,
      Would cry to a sailor, Go hang! 50
She loved not the savour of tar nor of pitch:
    Yet a tailor might scratch her where'er she did itch.
    Then to sea, boys, and let her go hang!
This is a scurvy tune too: but here's my comfort.
                     [*Drinks.*]

Caliban: Do not torment me:—O! 55
Stephano: What's the matter? Have we devils here? Do you
    put tricks upon's with savages and men of Ind, ha?
    I have not 'scaped drowning to be afeard now of your
    four legs; for it hath been said, As proper a man as
    ever went on four legs cannot make him give ground; 60
    and it shall be said so again while Stephano breathes
    at nostrils.
Caliban: The spirit torments me:—O!
Stephano: This is some monster of the isle with four legs,
    who hath got, as I take it, an ague. Where the devil 65
    should he learn our language? I will give him some

69   *trod on neat's leather:* wore shoes

74   *fit:* i.e., he is suffering an ague

75-76   *I will . . . hath him:* I will take as much as I can get for him.

77   *soundly:* in full

82   *cat:* a reference to the proverb, "Good liquor will make a cat speak."

85   *chaps:* jaws

88-89   *a most delicate/monster:* a most strangely constructed monster

92   *Amen:* Stop! That's enough for now.

96-97   *I have/no long spoon:* This is a reference to an old saying, " . . . he must have a long spoon who eats with the devil." In other words, it is best to keep your distance from the devil.

103   *very:* truly, really

104   *siege:* body excrement, stool; *moon-calf:* monster. This refers to the superstitious belief that monstrosities (imperfectly formed creatures) were the result of the negative influence of the moon; *vent:* excrete

relief, if it be but for that. If I can recover him and
keep him tame and get to Naples with him, he's a
present for any emperor that ever trod on neat's leather.

Caliban: Do not torment me, prithee; I'll bring my wood   70
home faster.

Stephano: He's in his fit now, and does not talk after the
wisest. He shall taste of my bottle: if he have never
drunk wine afore, it will go near to remove his fit.
If I can recover him and keep him tame, I will not take   75
too much for him; he shall pay for him that hath him,
and that soundly.

Caliban: Thou dost me yet but little hurt; thou wilt anon,
I know it by thy trembling: now Prosper works upon
thee.   80

Stephano: Come on your ways; open your mouth; here is
that which will give language to you, cat: open your
mouth; this will shake your shaking, I can tell you,
and that soundly: you cannot tell who's your friend:
open your chaps again.   85

Trinculo: I should know that voice: it should be—but he is
drowned; and these are devils:—O defend me!

Stephano: Four legs and two voices,—a most delicate
monster! His forward voice, now, is to speak well of
his friend; his backward voice is to utter foul speeches   90
and to detract. If all the wine in my bottle will recover
him, I will help his ague. Come:—Amen! I will pour
some in thy other mouth.

Trinculo: Stephano!

Stephano: Doth thy other mouth call me? Mercy, mercy!   95
This is a devil, and no monster: I will leave him; I have
no long spoon.

Trinculo: Stephano! If thou beest Stephano, touch me, and
speak to me; for I am Trinculo—be not afeard,—
thy good friend Trinculo.   100

Stephano: If thou beest Trinculo, come forth: I'll pull thee
by the lesser legs: if any be Trinculo's legs, these
are they. Thou art very Trinculo indeed! How camest
thou to be the siege of this moon-calf? Can he vent
Trinculos?   105

Trinculo: I took him to be killed with a thunderstroke. But

113   *constant:* steady

115   *brave:* handsome

119   *a butt of sack:* a cask or barrel of wine

127   *kiss the book:* take a drink from the bottle

135   *when time was:* once upon a time

137   *thy dog, and thy bush:* an old story tells that the Man in the Moon was banished there as punishment for having gathered wood with his dog on Sunday. On the moon with him there is said to be the dog and a thorny bush.

140   *By this good light:* An oath: by God; *shallow:* stupid

142   *Well drawn:* Caliban has had a full drink of wine.

143   *in good sooth:* cheers

art thou not drowned, Stephano? I hope, now, thou
art not drowned. Is the storm overblown? I hid me
under the dead moon-calf's gaberdine for fear of the
storm. And art thou living, Stephano? O Stephano, two 110
Neapolitans 'scaped!

Stephano: Prithee, do not turn me about; my stomach is
not constant.

Caliban: [*Aside.*] These be fine things, an if they be not
sprites.
That's a brave god, and bears celestial liquor: 115
I will kneel to him.

Stephano: How didst thou 'scape? How camest thou hither?
Swear by this bottle, how thou camest hither. I
escaped upon a butt of sack which the sailors heaved
o'erboard, by this bottle! Which I made of the bark 120
of a tree with my own hands, since I was cast ashore.

Caliban: I'll swear, upon that bottle, to be thy true subject;
for the liquor is not earthly.

Stephano: Here; swear, then, how thou escapedst.

Trinculo: Swum ashore, man, like a duck: I can swim like 125
a duck, I'll be sworn.

Stephano: Here, kiss the book. Though thou canst swim
like a duck, thou art made like a goose.

Trinculo: O Stephano, hast any more of this?

Stephano: The whole butt, man: my cellar is in a rock by 130
the sea-side, where my wine is hid. How now, moon-
calf! how does thine ague?

Caliban: Hast thou not dropped from heaven?

Stephano: Out o' the moon, I do assure thee: I was the man
i' the moon when time was. 135

Caliban: I have seen thee in her and I do adore thee: my
mistress show'd me thee, and thy dog, and thy bush.

Stephano: Come, swear to that: kiss the book. I will furnish it anon with new contents: swear.

Trinculo: By this good light, this is a very shallow monster! 140
I afeard of him! A very weak monster! The man i'
the moon! A most credulous monster! Well drawn,
monster, in good sooth!

Caliban: I'll show thee every fertile inch o' th' island;
And I will kiss thy foot: I prithee, be my god. 145

"I pledge to your teachings my master"

146   *perfidious:* treacherous

163   *crabs:* crab-apples

164   *pig-nuts:* plant roots

166   *marmoset:* a small monkey

168   *scamels:* probably a small sea bird

178   *trencher:* wooden plates

181   *hey-day:* Hurray!

Trinculo: By this light, a most perfidious and drunken
    monster! When's god's asleep, he'll rob his bottle.
Caliban: I'll kiss thy foot; I'll swear myself thy subject.
Stephano: Come on then; down, and swear.
Trinculo: I shall laugh myself to death at this puppy-headed   150
    monster. A most scurvy monster! I could find in my
    heart to beat him,—
Stephano: Come, kiss.
Trinculo: But that the poor monster's in drink. An abomi-
    nable monster!   155
Caliban: I'll show thee the best springs; I'll pluck thee
    berries;
  I'll fish for thee and get thee wood enough.
  A plague upon the tyrant that I serve!
  I'll bear him no more sticks, but follow thee,
  Thou wondrous man.   160
Trinculo: A most ridiculous monster, to make a wonder of
    a poor drunkard!
Caliban: I prithee, let me bring thee where crabs grow;
  And I with my long nails will dig thee pig-nuts;
  Show thee a jay's nest, and instruct thee how   165
  To snare the nimble marmoset; I'll bring thee
  To clustering filberts, and sometimes I'll get thee
  Young scamels from the rock. Wilt thou go with me?
Stephano: I prithee now, lead the way, without any more
    talking. Trinculo, the king and all our company else   170
    being drowned, we will inherit here: here; bear my
    bottle: fellow Trinculo, we'll fill him by and by again.
Caliban: [*Sings drunkenly.*]
    Farewell, master; farewell, farewell!
Trinculo: A howling monster; a drunken monster!
Caliban: *No more dams I'll make for fish;*   175
      Nor fetch in firing
      At requiring;
    Nor scrape trencher, nor wash dish:
      'Ban, 'Ban, Cacaliban
      Has a new master:—get a new man.   180
  Freedom, hey-day! Hey-day, freedom! Freedom,
  hey-day, freedom!
Stephano: O brave monster! Lead the way.   [*Exeunt.*]

Act 2, Scene 2: Activities

1. In your journals record your personal reactions to Caliban's opening speech lines 1–17.
   - What feelings does his soliloquy arouse in you?
   - How do these lines confirm, expand, or modify in any way your responses to Caliban in Act 1?

   Locate words, phrases, and/or images in the text of this speech that account for your responses. Discuss your thoughts and feelings with those of others in your group. Feel free to adjust your original entry.

2. Working with two classmates, take the parts of Caliban, Trinculo, and Stephano, in lines 18–105. Rehearse the scene segment in front of a small group of classmates and ask them to assess how effectively you conveyed the humour of this moment. Following their recommendations for ways in which you could make the situation more humorous, present the scene segment to a large group of classmates.

3. Ariel is not present in this scene and therefore is unable to tell Prospero what is happening. As a witness to the events of this scene, write a letter to Prospero, commenting upon Caliban's behaviour. Suggest possible explanations for Caliban's performance. You might add your advice to Prospero for ways to deal with him.

4. Imagine that you are someone who believes passionately in temperance (the non-use of alcohol). Improvise a short scene in which you appear before Caliban, Stephano, and Trinculo at this point in the play. What will you say? How might they respond? In a group of four, role-play your improvisation for other members of the class. Compare your improvisation with those of other groups.

5. Caliban is often addressed and referred to in this scene as a "monster". As a costume designer and/or make-up artist, decide how you would present this character. You might consider the illustrations of Caliban that appear in this edition before you make your decision. Draw an illustration or create a mask which expresses this character as you understand him at this point. In written or oral form, explain your rendering to an audience of your choice.

6. In groups, discuss Trinculo's idea of making money by displaying Caliban as some sort of freak in a show in Naples. What is your response to Trinculo's comment about human nature, lines 26–36? In your opinion, are people today attracted or appalled by side-shows? In a journal entry, write your views on the issue of side-shows. Before you begin, you might research show business explanations that have been provided for displaying human misery and affliction. The play *The Elephant Man* by Bernard Pomerance (Grove Press, 1979) offers one explanation.

Act 2: Consider the Whole Act

1. The characters in this act seem to view the island differently. Consider, once again, the responses of each one as he communicates them in this act. List the characters on one side of the sheet and beside each name list his responses. Use as many actual quotes as you can find to illustrate their viewpoints. Is it possible to group these characters from what you have discovered?

2. Imagine you are filming a scene segment from this act. Create a storyboard (see page 50, activity 4) to plan the camera shots for this scene.

As you plan the drawings, consider details such as the following:
- What are the background features for each shot?
- Will the shots be long, close-up or medium shots (showing about two-thirds of the subject) or a tracking shot – a shot where the camera moves to show the movement of the subject.

Share your storyboards with classmates and see if they can identify the dialogue which accompanies the various camera shots.

3. While Caliban may be one step from being a beast, he is nonetheless human. What is your opinion of Prospero's treatment of him? As Caliban, write a letter to Prospero protesting your current treatment. You may wish to write your letter as a journal entry or share it with others in a group.

4. Stephano and Trinculo are being interviewed about where they are. They make little sense and are asked to draw a map of their version of the island. What kind of map might they draw? What sorts of sights might they locate on it? What kinds of things would they see, or think they saw? In a group of three, question Stephano and Trinculo about their map so that you might get a clearer impression of where they are and how they got there. Use as many of the specific references from the play as you can. How believable is their version of the island?

5. Choose one character in either scene for whom you know the perfect modern-day actor to play the character's role. In pairs, role-play a situation in which one of you, playing the part of the casting director, tries to convince this actor to accept the role. Present your conversation to classmates.

6. Recalling Gonzalo's commonwealth speech (Act 2, Scene 1) and considering your response to Antonio,

Gonzalo, and Caliban, in a group discuss your opinions about the following:

- What kind of people would need to populate Gonzalo's state for it to survive and flourish?
- What threats to its survival would Antonio and Caliban pose? Why?
- What attempts do you know about where one or more people have attempted to create a society similar to the one Gonzalo envisions? What happened?

7. Prospero's island is simply an island; there are very few clues to its exact location in the play. However, there are hints that it could be Bermuda or an island in the Mediterranean sea. If you could identify the island for this play, which one would you choose? Create a travel brochure which describes and shows what the island looks like. You may wish to add details to your brochure as the play unfolds. Display the brochure for classmates to see.

For the next scene . . .

Think of a few well-known love stories. Why do you think that in most love stories there is an obstacle to be overcome before the lovers can come together? Using some of the love stories with which you are familiar, jot down your ideas in a journal entry.

Act 3, Scene 1

In this scene . . .

Ferdinand enters bearing the wood that Prospero has
ordered him to pile. Miranda arrives and soon the
two confess their love for each other. Prospero, hidden
nearby, oversees all that happens. When Miranda
and Ferdinand agree to become husband and wife,
Prospero expresses his fatherly delight in their union.

1-2   *and their . . . off:* the delight we take from some kinds of labour compensates for difficulties we must undergo in carrying them out

3-4   *most poor . . . ends:* the most lowly of tasks or occupations may lead to the most glorious achievements or final results

5   *odious:* hateful

6   *quickens:* gives life to

8   *crabbed:* irritable and ill-tempered

11   *sore injunction:* harsh command

13   *I forget:* Ferdinand remembers that he must continue his work

15   *Most busy . . . it:* There are various interpretations of this line. One understanding is: Ferdinand's "sweet thoughts" (line 14) are most active when he is carrying out his task and therefore comfort him in his labour.

18-19   *when this . . . you:* This line takes the form of a conceit (an exaggerated metaphor) which refers to the resinous drops which issue from burning wood.

Act 3, Scene 1

Before Prospero's cell.

Enter Ferdinand, bearing a log.

Ferdinand: There be some sports are painful, and their labour
    Delight in them sets off: some kinds of baseness
    Are nobly undergone and most poor matters
    Point to rich ends. This my mean task
    Would be as heavy to me as odious, but   5
    The mistress which I serve quickens what's dead,
    And makes my labours pleasures: O, she is
    Ten times more gentle than her father's crabbed,
    And he's composed of harshness. I must remove
    Some thousands of these logs, and pile them up,   10
    Upon a sore injunction: my sweet mistress
    Weeps when she sees me work, and says, such baseness
    Had never like executor. I forget:
    But these sweet thoughts do even refresh my labours,
    Most busy, least when I do it.
    [*Enter Miranda; and Prospero at a distance, unseen.*]
Miranda: Alas, now, pray you,   15
    Work not so hard: I would the lightning had
    Burnt up those logs that you are enjoin'd to pile!
    Pray, set it down, and rest you: when this burns,
    'Twill weep for having wearied you. My father
    Is hard at study; pray now, rest yourself;   20
    He's safe for these three hours.
Ferdinand: O most dear mistress,
    The sun will set before I shall discharge
    What I must strive to do.
Miranda: If you'll sit down,
    I'll bear your logs the while: pray, give me that;
    I'll carry it to the pile.

31 *Poor worm:* an affectionate term meaning "my dearest child" or "my dear, you are blind in your innocence"

32 *visitation:* visit, the word was also used to mean an attack of disease upon the body. The word continues the metaphor of the preceding line.

36 *Miranda:* The name is also a Latin word meaning "worthy of admiration."

37 *hest:* command

40 *with best regard:* carefully

41-42 *hath into . . . ear:* has charmed my hearing, i.e., I have been charmed by their sweet words

44-46 *but some . . . foil:* but always there was something about her that flawed her beauty; *owed:* possessed; *foil:* opposite

47 *peerless:* without equal

52-53 *how features . . . of:* I do not know what people living elsewhere look like.

57 *prattle:* babble; talk in a childish or silly way

Ferdinand: No, precious creature;   25
  I had rather crack my sinews, break my back,
  Than you should such dishonour undergo,
  While I sit lazy by.
Miranda: It would become me
  As well as it does you: and I should do it
  With much more ease; for my good will is to it,   30
  And yours it is against.
Prospero: Poor worm, thou art infected!
  This visitation shows it.
Miranda: You look wearily.
Ferdinand: No, noble mistress; 'tis fresh morning with me
  When you are by at night. I do beseech you,—
  Chiefly that I might set it in my prayers,—   35
  What is your name?
Miranda: Miranda—O my father,
  I have broke your hest to say so!
Ferdinand: Admired Miranda!
  Indeed the top of admiration! Worth
  What's dearest to the world! Full many a lady
  I have eyed with best regard, and many a time   40
  The harmony of their tongues hath into bondage
  Brought my too diligent ear: for several virtues
  Have I liked several women; never any
  With so full soul, but some defect in her
  Did quarrel with the noblest grace she owed,   45
  And put it to the foil: but you, O you,
  So perfect and so peerless, are created
  Of every creature's best!
Miranda: I do not know
  One of my sex; no woman's face remember,
  Save, from my glass, mine own; nor have I seen   50
  More that I may call men than you, good friend,
  And my dear father: how features are abroad,
  I am skilless of; but, by my modesty,
  The jewel in my dower, I would not wish
  Any companion in the world but you;   55
  Nor can imagination form a shape,
  Besides yourself, to like of. But I prattle

58   *precepts:* orders

59   *in my condition:* in rank

62-63   *than to . . . mouth:* than to allow a fly to rest on my lips

69   *crown what . . . event:* Let happy events follow what I say.

70-71   *If hollowly . . . mischief:* If I am not sincere in what I say, then let the greatest blessing fate holds in store for me be turned to misfortune.

78-79   *What I desire . . . want:* Miranda says that she will die if she does not possess the love of Ferdinand

79   *trifling:* idle talk

80-81   *And all . . . shows:* The more I try to conceal my love, the more obvious it becomes.

81   *bashful cunning:* shyness that pretends to conceal the love she has for Ferdinand

89   *As bondage e'er of freedom:* as happily as ever a slave accepted freedom

Something too wildly, and my father's precepts
I therein do forget.
Ferdinand: I am, in my condition,
A prince, Miranda; I do think, a king;   60
I would, not so!—and would no more endure
This wooden slavery than to suffer
The flesh-fly blow my mouth. Hear my soul speak:
The very instant that I saw you, did
My heart fly to your service; there resides,   65
To make me slave to it; and for your sake
Am I this patient log-man.
Miranda: Do you love me?
Ferdinand: O heaven, O earth, bear witness to this sound,
And crown what I profess with kind event,
If I speak true! If hollowly, invert   70
What best is boded me to mischief! I,
Beyond all limit of what else i' the world,
Do love, prize, honour you.
Miranda: I am a fool
To weep at what I am glad of.
Prospero: Fair encounter
Of two most rare affections! Heavens rain grace   75
On that which breeds between 'em!
Ferdinand: Wherefore weep you?
Miranda: At mine unworthiness, that dare not offer
What I desire to give; and much less take
What I shall die to want. But this is trifling;
And all the more it seeks to hide itself,   80
The bigger bulk it shows. Hence, bashful cunning!
And prompt me, plain and holy innocence!
I am your wife, if you will marry me;
If not, I'll die your maid: to be your fellow
You may deny me; but I'll be your servant,   85
Whether you will or no.
Ferdinand: My mistress, dearest;
And I thus humble ever.
Miranda: My husband, then?
Ferdinand: Ay, with a heart as willing
As bondage e'er of freedom: here's my hand.

93   *withal:* who are surprised with all that has happened

94   *book:* Prospero's book of magic

96   *appertaining:* i.e., related to my plan

Miranda: And mine, with my heart in't: and now farewell   90
 Till half an hour hence.
Ferdinand: A thousand thousand!
   [Exeunt Ferdinand and Miranda severally.]
Prospero: So glad of this as they I cannot be,
 Who are surprised withal; but my rejoicing
 At nothing can be more. I'll to my book;
 For yet, ere supper-time, must I perform   95
 Much business appertaining.   *[Exit.]*

Father = not ok yet.

Act 3, Scene 1: Activities

1. In his first speech in this scene, lines 1–14, Ferdinand criticizes Prospero because of the work he must do. In the previous scene, Act 2, Scene 2, lines 1–16, Caliban also curses Prospero for having to perform the same task, that is, piling wood. With a partner, complete the following:
   - Imagine a meeting between Ferdinand and Caliban, at the wood pile, and write a script for their dialogue. What would they say about Prospero?
   - Role-play their conversation for an audience of classmates.

2. Within the few minutes it takes to perform this scene, Ferdinand and Miranda fall in love and decide to become husband and wife. In your journal, record your reaction to this event. Do sudden romances occur in real life? How do you respond to this scene? How do you think a theatre audience might respond to it? Discuss your responses to these questions in a group.

3. In a group, discuss how you might stage this scene so that Prospero is seen and heard by the audience, but not by Miranda and Ferdinand. Consider the following:
   - Would Prospero address the audience or speak only to himself?
   - Would he move about the stage or remain in one position?
   - Where would you place the two lovers in relation to Prospero?
   As the director for this scene, make an entry in your director's log, explaining how you would stage this segment of the play.

4. As Ferdinand or Miranda, write about your feelings for the other. You might express yourself in a letter to a close friend, a poem, or a song. You may wish to quote lines from the text in your expression.

For the next scene . . .

In groups, recall movies, books, and/or television programs in which drunkenness has been used as a source of humour. For what purpose might the writers have chosen drunks to provide comic effect? Did any of the writers use "the drunk" to make a statement about human behaviour? Discuss your ideas.

Act 3, Scene 2

In this scene . . .

Caliban, Stephano, and Trinculo are now quite drunk.
Trinculo begins to mock Caliban, but Stephano
comes to the monster's defence, warning Trinculo to
be more civil towards the creature. When Ariel,
invisible to the three, enters upon the scene, he
mischievously provokes the brawling trio into an
all-out fight.

Caliban begins to outline for Stephano and Trinculo
his plan of action for murdering Prospero and taking
over control of the island. The three are soon distracted
from their murderous conspiracy, however, as Ariel
begins to play "sounds and sweet airs" upon his pipe.
The three decide to follow this strange music to
discover its source and agree to return later to carry
out their work.

2-3   *therefore bear up, and/board 'em:* Stephano is using sailors' language to invite his companions to drink.

4   *the folly of this island:* the circumstances of this island cause such foolish things to happen as Stephano finding himself having his own servant.

13-14   *off/and on:* more or less

15   *standard:* flag carrier

16   *if you list:* just listen to that Stephano exaggerate or carry on

18   *lie:* a pun: to tell a lie, to lie drunk upon the ground

24-25   *in case/ . . . constable:* courageous enough to attack a policeman

25   *deboshed:* debauched, drunken

Scene 2

Another part of the island.

*Enter Caliban, Stephano, and
Trinculo.*

Stephano: Tell not me:—when the butt is out, we will drink
water; not a drop before: therefore bear up, and
board 'em. Servant-monster, drink to me.

Trinculo: Servant-monster! the folly of this island! They say
there's but five upon this isle: we are three of them;   5
if th' other two be brained like us, the state totters.

Stephano: Drink, servant-monster, when I bid thee: thy eyes
are almost set in thy head.

Trinculo: Where should they be set else? He were a brave
monster indeed, if they were set in his tail.   10

Stephano: My man-monster hath drown'd his tongue in sack:
for my part, the sea cannot drown me; I swam, ere
I could recover the shore, five and thirty leagues off
and on. By this light, thou shalt be my lieutenant,
monster, or my standard.   15

Trinculo: Your lieutenant, if you list; he's no standard.

Stephano: We'll not run, Monsieur Monster.

Trinculo: Nor go neither; but you'll lie, like dogs, and yet
say nothing neither.

Stephano: Moon-calf, speak once in thy life, if thou beest a   20
good moon-calf.

Caliban: How does thy honour? Let me lick thy shoe. I'll
not serve him; he is not valiant.

Trinculo: Thou liest, most ignorant monster: I am in case
to justle a constable. Why, thou deboshed fish, thou,   25
was there ever man a coward that hath drunk so much
sack as I to-day? Wilt thou tell a monstrous lie, being
but half a fish and half a monster?

31   *natural:* an idiot

34   *the next tree:* Stephano threatens to hang Trinculo if he doesn't
      stop taunting Caliban.

48   *supplant:* remove

57   *compassed?:* brought about; happen

59   *I'll yield him thee sleep:* I'll bring you to him while he is sleeping.

62   *pied:* a reference to the multicoloured clothes of Trinculo,
      the traditional dress of the court jester; *ninny's:* simpleton;
      patch: The jester's clothes were also made of patches of
      colourful materials sewn together in random patterns.

66   *quick freshes:* fresh water

Caliban: Lo, how he mocks me! Wilt thou let him, my lord?
Trinculo: "Lord" quoth he! That a monster should be such   30
    a natural!
Caliban: Lo, lo, again! Bite him to death, I prithee.
Stephano: Trinculo, keep a good tongue in your head: if
    you prove a mutineer,—the next tree! The poor
    monster's my subject, and he shall not suffer indignity.   35
Caliban: I thank my noble lord. Wilt thou be pleased to
    hearken once again to the suit I made to thee?
Stephano: Marry, will I: kneel and repeat it; I will stand,
    and so shall Trinculo.
    [*Enter Ariel, invisible.*]
Caliban: As I told thee before, I am subject to a tyrant, a   40
    sorcerer, that by his cunning hath cheated me of the
    island.
Ariel: Thou liest.
Caliban: Thou liest, thou jesting monkey, thou:
    I would my valiant master would destroy thee!   45
    I do not lie.
Stephano: Trinculo, if you trouble him any more in's tale,
    by this hand, I will supplant some of your teeth.
Trinculo: Why, I said nothing.
Stephano: Mum, then, and no more. Proceed.   50
Caliban: I say, by sorcery he got this isle;
    From me he got it. If thy greatness will
    Revenge it on him,—for I know thou darest,
    But this thing dare not,—
Stephano: That's most certain.   55
Caliban: Thou shalt be lord of it and I'll serve thee.
Stephano: How now shall this be compassed? Canst thou
    bring me to the party?
Caliban: Yea, yea, my lord: I'll yield him thee asleep.
    Where thou mayest knock a nail into his head.   60
Ariel: Thou liest; thou canst not.
Caliban: What a pied ninny's this! Thou scurvy patch!
    I do beseech thy greatness, give him blows
    And take his bottle from him: when that's gone,
    He shall drink naught but brine; for I'll not show him   65
    Where the quick freshes are.

69   *stock-fish:* dried cod fish

76   *give me the lie:* accuse me of lying

79   *murrain:* a deadly or infectious disease

89   *paunch:* pierce

90   *wezand:* throat

92   *sot:* a foolish person, a person who is constantly drunk

96   *deck:* display, decorate

99   *nonpareil:* peerless, without an equal

Stephano: Trinculo, run into no further danger: interrupt
    the monster one word further, and, by this hand, I'll
    turn my mercy out o'doors, and make a stock-fish
    of thee.   70

Trinculo: Why, what did I? I did nothing. I'll go farther
    off.

Stephano: Didst thou not say he lied?

Ariel: Thou liest.

Stephano: Do I so? Take thou that. [*Beats Trinculo.*] As you   75
    like this, give me the lie another time.

Trinculo: I did not give the lie. Out o' your wits and hearing
    too? A pox o' your bottle! This can sack and drinking
    do. A murrain on your monster, and the devil take your
    fingers.   80

Caliban: Ha, ha, ha!

Stephano: Now, forward with your tale.—Prithee, stand
    farther off.

Caliban: Beat him enough: after a little time
    I'll beat him too.

Stephano: Stand farther.—Come, proceed.   85

Caliban: Why, as I told thee, 'tis a custom with him
    I' th' afternoon to sleep: there thou mayst brain him
    Having first seized his books; or with a log
    Batter his skull, or paunch him with a stake,
    Or cut his wezand with thy knife. Remember   90
    First to possess his books; for without them
    He's but a sot, as I am, nor hath not
    One spirit to command: they all do hate him
    As rootedly as I. Burn but his books.
    He has brave utensils,—for so he calls them,—   95
    Which, when he has a house, he'll deck withal.
    And that most deeply to consider is
    The beauty of his daughter; he himself
    Calls her a nonpareil: I never saw a woman,
    But only Sycorax my dam and she;   100
    But she as far surpasseth Sycorax
    As great'st does least.

Stephano: Is it so brave a lass?

Caliban: Ay, lord; she will become thy bed, I warrant,

104   *brood:* family of children

107   *viceroys:* governors who represent the king

116   *jocund:* happy, joyous
117   *while-ere?:* just now
118   *do reason:* do anything that is reasonable
120   *flout:* mock, insult; *scout:* jeer, laugh at

124   *this same?:* the same tune
125-126 *the picture/of Nobody:* This is an allusion to the picture of a
         man with a head, legs, and arms, but without a body. The
         picture appeared in the title page of a comedy entitled
         "Nobody and Some-body" published in the early 1600s.
128   *take't as thou list:* take whatever shape you please

136   *twangling:* a word imitating the sounds of stringed instruments

And bring thee forth brave brood.
Stephano: Monster, I will kill this man: his daughter and I 105
    will be king and queen,—save our Graces!—and Trin-
    culo and thyself shall be viceroys. Dost thou like the
    plot, Trinculo?
Trinculo: Excellent.
Stephano: Give me thy hand: I am sorry I beat thee; but 110
    while thou livest, keep a good tongue in thy head.
Caliban: Within this half hour will he be asleep:
    Wilt thou destroy him then?
Stephano: Ay, on mine honour.
Ariel: This will I tell my master.
Caliban: Thou makest me merry: I am full of pleasure: 115
    Let us be jocund: will you troll the catch
    You taught me but while-ere?
Stephano: At thy request, monster, I will do reason, any
    reason.—Come on, Trinculo, let us sing.
    [*Sings.*] *Flout 'em and scout 'em,* 120
            And scout 'em and flout 'em;
                Thought is free.
Caliban: That's not the tune.
                [*Ariel plays the tune on a tabor and pipe.*]
Stephano: What is this same?
Trinculo: This is the tune of our catch, played by the picture 125
    of Nobody.
Stephano: If thou beest a man, show thyself in thy likeness:
    if thou beest a devil, take't as thou list.
Trinculo: O, forgive me my sins!
Stephano: He that dies pays all debts: I defy thee. 130
    Mercy upon us!
Caliban: Art thou afeard?
Stephano: No, monster, not I.
Caliban: Be not afeard; the isle is full of noises.
    Sounds and sweet airs, that give delight, and hurt not. 135
    Sometimes a thousand twangling instruments
    Will hum about mine ears; and sometimes voices,
    That, if I then had waked after long sleep,
    Will make me sleep again: and then, in dreaming,
    The clouds methought would open, and show riches 140

150   *taborer:* one who plays a little drum

Ready to drop upon me; that, when I waked,
  I cried to dream again.
Stephano: This will prove a brave kingdom to me, where I
  shall have my music for nothing.
Caliban: When Prospero is destroyed.   145
Stephano: That shall be by and by: I remember the story.
Trinculo: The sound is going away; let's follow it, and after
  do our work.
Stephano: Lead, monster, we'll follow. I would I could see
  this taborer; he lays it on.   150
Trinculo: Wilt come? I'll follow, Stephano.   [*Exeunt.*]

Act 3, Scene 2: Activities

1. a) As the director, how would you stage the first 84 lines
   of this scene to develop the comedy most effectively? Rehearse the scene segment with volunteers
   from your group and present it to your classmates.
   Before you make your presentation, research and/or
   recall well-known comic routines.

   b) As a newspaper reporter, write a review of the above
   comic performance.

2. Examine the words Caliban uses in this scene and his
   style of speech. How is his language different from
   that of Stephano and Trinculo? In a group discuss your
   ideas about Caliban's character. Does the language
   he uses in this scene affect your sense of him? Explain
   your response.

3. Imagine that you have been asked to create a music
   video for Caliban's speech, lines 134–142. What
   music and actions would you use? Write out your ideas.
   If video equipment is available to you, produce a
   music video for the class to view.

4. Caliban and Stephano's plot to murder Prospero parallels Antonio and Sebastian's murder plot in Act 2,
   Scene 1. Write a short essay in which you describe the
   similarities and differences between these two plots.
   Offer your opinions about the chances of success for
   either scheme. Share your written work with classmates.

5. At the end of this scene, Ariel's music distracts the
   conspirators from murdering Prospero. In your journal,
   recall an experience you have had in which music had
   a strong influence on your behaviour and/or mood.
   How do you think it is possible for music to create such
   an effect?

For the next scene . . .

Recall an experience you had in which you thought you had succeeded in getting away with something only to be punished for it at a later date. How did you react when you were found out? Write about your experience in your journal. If you cannot recall such a situation, imagine how you might feel about such an experience.

Act 3, Scene 3

In this scene . . .

Exhausted from their long search for Ferdinand, Gonzalo, and Alonso stop to rest. Alonso admits he has given up hope of finding his son alive. Antonio and Sebastian realize that they will soon have another chance to murder the two men. Suddenly they hear strange music. Prospero enters invisibly along with several strange shapes bearing a banquet table laden with food. They bid the men to eat and then depart. Just as the men are about to do so, Ariel enters, disguised, and causes the food to disappear. He then delivers a speech to Alonso, Sebastian, and Antonio in which he tells them they are being punished for what they did to Prospero and Miranda. Ariel disappears, and, Prospero, who has watched the action unobserved, is pleased with what has happened. Alonso leaves to find Ferdinand and to die beside him, and Antonio and Sebastian leave to find and fight the spirits. Gonzalo and Adrian follow the three to prevent them from harming themselves while in this frenzied mood.

1   *by'r lakin:* by our Lady (the Virgin Mary)

2   *maze trod:* Gonzalo speaks of the intricate network of paths on which they have been wandering. A maze is a labyrinth.

3   *forth-rights and meanders:* straight and winding paths. The Meander is a winding river in Asia Minor

5   *attach'd with:* in a state of

8   *for my flatterer:* Alonso says he will no longer deceive himself with false hope.

10   *frustrate:* useless and frustrating

12   *for one repulse:* because you failed in your first attempt

14   *thoroughly:* carry out fully, i.e., we will complete the murder

Scene 3

Another part of the island.

*Enter Alonso, Sebastian, Antonio,
Gonzalo, Adrian, Francisco, and
others.*

Gonzalo: By'r lakin, I can go no further, sir;
  My old bones ache: here's a maze trod, indeed,
  Through forth-rights and meanders! By your patience,
  I needs must rest me.
Alonso: Old lord, I cannot blame thee,
  Who am myself attach'd with weariness,   5
  To the dulling of my spirits: sit down, and rest.
  Even here I will put off my hope, and keep it
  No longer for my flatterer: he is drown'd
  Whom thus we stray to find; and the sea mocks
  Our frustrate search on land. Well, let him go.   10
Antonio: [*Aside to Sebastian.*] I am right glad that he's so
    out of hope.
  Do not, for one repulse, forgo the purpose
  That you resolved to effect.
Sebastian: [*Aside to Antonio.*] The next advantage
  Will we take throughly.
Antonio: [*Aside to Sebastian.*] Let it be to-night:
  For, now they are oppress'd with travel, they   15
  Will not, nor cannot, use such vigilance
  As when they are fresh.
Sebastian: [*Aside to Antonio.*] I say, to-night: no more.
                    [*Solemn and strange music.*]
Alonso: What harmony is this?—My good friends, hark!
Gonzalo: Marvellous sweet music!
  [*Enter Prospero above, invisible. Enter several strange Shapes,
    bringing in a banquet; they dance about it with gentle
    actions of salutation; and, inviting the King, etc., to eat,
    they depart.*]

21 *A living drollery:* a "drollery" was a type of dramatic entertainment in which the actors were dolls or perhaps puppet-like characters.

22 *unicorns:* a fabled animal represented as a horse with a horn projecting from the forehead

23 *the phœnix' throne:* The phoenix was a mythical bird who lived for 500 years. When it was time to die, the phoenix would build a funeral pyre and after setting it on fire she was consumed to ashes. From these ashes, however, a new phoenix sprang forth. The "throne" refers to the funeral pyre.

26-27 *travellers ne'er . . . 'em:* Travellers returning from voyages to far-away places would return home with exaggerated and sometimes false tales of their experience.

36 *muse:* wonder at

38-39 *Although they . . . discourse:* Although they do not speak yet, they communicate clearly by their actions.

39 *Praise in departing:* This is part of the proverb which says, "Do not praise your host too soon; wait to see how the occasion will end." Prospero, in his aside, cautions them to wait till the end before praising their courteous providers of this banquet.

44-45 *mountaineers/Dew-lapp'd like bulls:* This is a reference to a people who lived in the moist valleys of the Alpine mountains, many of whom suffered from a goitre condition, i.e., a visible swelling at the front of their necks caused by an enlarged thyroid gland condition. It is similar in appearance to the skin that hangs from the throats of cows.

46 *Wallets of flesh?:* This is a continuation of the comparison in lines 44-45. "Wallets" is a form of the word "wattle," the skin that hangs from the neck of a turkey.

47 *Whose heads . . . breasts?:* This is a reference to Elizabethan sailors' accounts of a strange race of men without conventional heads but with eyes located in their shoulders and mouths in their breasts.

48 *Each putter-out . . . one:* This is a reference to a business practice during the Elizabethan age. Travellers would deposit a sum of money in London before their departure. If they returned safely from their voyage, they would collect five times the amount; if they did not return, the money was forfeited.

Alonso: Give us kind keepers, heavens!—What were these?　20
Sebastian: A living drollery. Now I will believe
　　That there are unicorns; that in Arabia
　　There is one tree, the phœnix' throne; one phœnix
　　At this hour reigning there.
Antonio:　　　　　　　　　I'll believe both;
　　And what does else want credit, come to me,　　　25
　　And I'll be sworn 'tis true: travellers ne'er did lie,
　　Though fools at home condemn 'em.
Gonzalo:　　　　　　　　　If in Naples
　　I should report this now, would they believe me?
　　If I should say, I saw such islanders—
　　For, certes, these are people of the island—　　30
　　Who, though they are of monstrous shape, yet note,
　　Their manners are more gentle-kind than of
　　Our human generation you shall find
　　Many, nay, almost any.
Prospero: [*Aside.*]　　　　Honest lord,
　　Thou hast said well; for some of you there present　35
　　Are worse than devils.
Alonso:　　　　　　　I cannot too much muse
　　Such shapes, such gesture and such sound, expressing,—
　　Although they want the use of tongue,—a kind
　　Of excellent dumb discourse.
Prospero: [*Aside.*]　　　　Praise in departing.
Francisco: They vanish'd strangely.
Sebastian:　　　　　　　No matter, since　　40
　　They have left their viands behind; for we have
　　　stomachs.—
　　Will't please you taste of what is here?
Alonso:　　　　　　Not I.
Gonzalo: Faith, sir, you need not fear. When we were boys,
　　Who would believe that there were mountaineers
　　Dew-lapp'd like bulls, whose throats had hanging at 'em　45
　　Wallets of flesh? Or that there were such men
　　Whose heads stood in their breasts? Which now we find
　　Each putter-out on five for one will bring us
　　Good warrant of.
Alonso:　　　　I will stand to and feed,
　　Although my last: no matter, since I feel　　　50

51   *The best is past:* All that made life worth living has been taken from me.

Stage direction – *harpy:* a mythical creature having a woman's face and trunk and a bird's feathers, wings, and talons; *quaint device:* a peculiar and clever stage device

54   *That hath to instrument:* whose responsibility it is to order the course of events

55   *never-surfeited:* insatiable; never having enough victims to swallow

59-60   *hang and . . . selves:* When driven to madness, men hang and drown themselves.

62   *are temper'd:* are made

65   *dowle:* feather

66   *invulnerable:* incapable of being wounded

67   *massy:* heavy

70   *supplant:* displace

71   *which hath requit it:* which has repaid you for your sin by the calamities you are now suffering

74   *Incensed:* enraged, made angry

76   *bereft [of]:* bereaved of, suffer the loss of

77   *Lingering perdition:* Complete ruin will come upon you in slow degrees gradually consuming you in continued suffering.

81-82   *is nothing . . . ensuing:* There is no alternative to or escape from the anger of the supreme powers except repentance and amendment of your lives.

Stage direction – *mocks and mows:* mocking looks and grimaces

The best is past. Brother, my lord the duke,
Stand to and do as we.
[*Thunder and lightning. Enter Ariel, like a harpy; claps his
wings upon the table; and, with a quaint device, the
banquet vanishes.*]
Ariel: You are three men of sin, whom Destiny,—
That hath to instrument this lower world
And what is in't—the never-surfeited sea   55
Hath caused to belch up you; and on this island
Where man doth not inhabit;—you 'mongst men
Being most unfit to live. I have made you mad;
And even with such-like valour men hang and drown
Their proper selves. [*Alonso, Sebastian, etc., draw their
swords.*]   You fools! I and my fellows   60
Are ministers of Fate: the elements,
Of whom your swords are temper'd, may as well
Wound the loud winds or with bemock'd-at stabs
Kill the still-closing waters, as diminish
One dowle that's in my plume: my fellow-ministers   65
Are like invulnerable. If you could hurt,
Your swords are now too massy for your strengths,
And will not be uplifted. But remember—
For that's my business to you—that you three
From Milan did supplant good Prospero;   70
Exposed unto the sea, which hath requit it,
Him and his innocent child: for which foul deed
The powers, delaying, not forgetting, have
Incensed the seas and shores, yea, all the creatures,
Against your peace. Thee of thy son, Alonso,   75
They have bereft; and do pronounce by me
Lingering perdition,—worse than any death
Can be at once,—shall step by step attend
You and your ways; whose wraths to guard you from—
Which here, in this most desolate isle, else falls   80
Upon your heads—is nothing but heart-sorrow
And a clear life ensuing.
[*He vanishes in thunder; then, to soft music, enter the Shapes
again, and dance, with mocks and mows, and carrying
out the table.*]

84   *devouring:* fascinating

85   *bated:* omitted, left out

87-88   *observation strange . . . done:* and so too did my lower spirit-servants carry out their duties perfectly

96   *billows:* the surges or swell of the sea

99   *bass my trespass:* (the thunder) spoke to me of my sin against Prospero

100   *ooze:* the mud on the ocean floor

101   *plummets sounded:* a lead weight used to measure (sound) the depth of the sea

105   *Like poison . . . after:* like poison which, although it doesn't have an immediate effect, nevertheless produces its disastrous results over a long period of time

107   *That are of suppler joints:* Gonzalo asks Adrian and Francisco, who in their youth are more physically fit than he, to follow the others as they continue their wanderings over the island.

108   *ecstasy:* madness

109   *May now provoke them to:* to the deeds their madness may urge them to commit.

Prospero: Bravely the figure of this harpy hast thou
  Perform'd, my Ariel; a grace it had, devouring:
  Of my instruction hast thou nothing bated   85
  In what thou hadst to say: so, with good life
  And observation strange, my meaner ministers
  Their several kinds have done. My high charms work,
  And these mine enemies are all knit up
  In their distractions: they now are in my power;   90
  And in these fits I leave them, while I visit
  Young Ferdinand,—whom they suppose is drown'd,—
  And his and mine loved darling.   [*Exit above.*]
Gonzalo: I' the name of something holy, sir, why stand you
  In this strange stare?
Alonso: O, it is monstrous, monstrous!   95
  Methought the billows spoke, and told me of it;
  The winds did sing it to me; and the thunder,
  That deep and dreadful organ-pipe, pronounced
  The name of Prosper: it did bass my trespass.
  Therefore my son i' the ooze is bedded; and   100
  I'll seek him deeper than e'er plummets sounded,
  And with him there lie mudded.   [*Exit.*]
Sebastian: But one fiend at a time,
  I'll fight their legions o'er.
Antonio: I'll be thy second.
           [*Exeunt Sebastian and Antonio.*]
Gonzalo: All three of them are desperate; their great guilt,
  Like poison given to work a great time after,   105
  Now 'gins to bite the spirits, I do beseech you,
  That are of suppler joints, follow them swiftly,
  And hinder them from what this ecstasy
  May now provoke them to.
Adrian: Follow, I pray you. [*Exeunt.*]

Act 3, Scene 3: Activities

1. How do Antonio, Sebastian, and Alonso react to being found out? Was their response similar to or different from the one you provided to the question asked in For the next scene . . ., page 119? Remember that the crime of ousting Prospero and abandoning him to the sea happened twelve years before the banquet scene.

   In a group discuss the following:
   • Is it fair that the trio be punished so many years after their crime?
   • Is the punishment appropriate for the crime? Why or why not?

2. Although Gonzalo did not hear Ariel's speech to the three men of sin, he, nevertheless, seems to know that Alonso, Antonio, and Sebastian are affected by their "great guilt". Using Gonzalo's lines beginning, "All three of them are desperate . . ." (line 104) complete the diary entry Gonzalo might write at this moment in the play. Predict what might happen to Gonzalo and share your ideas with a partner.

3. In a modern production of *The Tempest*, it would be possible to have highly inventive props and sets to accompany Ariel's speech, lines 53–82. What visuals would you choose to support Ariel's words of accusation? Describe in writing the visual effects. You may wish to include sketches with your description. You may prefer to use slides to create the effects.

4. As Alonso, write a letter to your daughter Claribel, telling her about what has happened since you left her wedding celebrations. Describe your emotional state, and explain what you are planning to do to rectify your situation.

5. Research the characteristics and the role of the harpy in Greek mythology. You might begin your investigation by reading the myth, *The Quest of Jason for the Golden Fleece*. Prepare an oral or written report in which you explain the part of the harpy and comment upon the appropriateness of Shakespeare's choosing the harpy image for the banquet scene. Present your report to the class.

6. a) Imagine that you have been caught in a time warp. You are now a part of this scene but don't know what events happened prior to the vanishing of the banquet. How would you respond to the following questions:
   - What is going on? What happened before this point?
   - What do you think of the people around you?
   - Which character(s) would you want to get to know? Why?
   - Which characters do you want to stay away from? Why?
   - Who do you speak to first and why?
   - How do these people respond to you?
   - Where are you and how do you feel about this location?

   b) When you are returned to your own world, you decide to submit a report of your adventure to the publisher of a newspaper or magazine. To which publication do you consider making your submission? Who might believe your story? Write your report and share it with classmates.

Act 3: Consider the Whole Act

1. To this point in the play we have been following each of the three separated parties from the shipwreck of the opening scene. With a partner identify the three different categories of passengers and discuss your responses to the following questions:
   - What physical discomforts, and (where applicable) what spiritual and emotional distress has each suffered?
   - What do you think is Prospero's purpose in having each party undergo these experiences?
   Share your observations with classmates.

2. If you could give advice to one character in this act, who would you choose? Why? What advice would you give? Choose a moment in one of the scenes at which you might offer your advice. Write your advice in a speech and share it with classmates, explaining where you would insert it.

3. As a musical adviser, select a speech or scene segment from this act for which you feel musical accompaniment would be appropriate. What type of music would you select? Prepare an audio tape to share with classmates. Be prepared to defend your choice of music, using the text to support your opinion.

4. Imagine that you are in charge of publicity for a production of *The Tempest*. You have purchased space for a two-page newspaper spread to advertise Act 3. What moment(s) from this act will you highlight? Design a layout of the spread, indicating what kinds of illustrations, captions, and text copy you will include.

5. Identify in history or your contemporary world a person who is considered to be a person of sin such as Antonio, Sebastian, and Alonso. As Prospero, decide how you

would confront him/her. What would you say and do? What might the reaction of your "criminal" be?

Present a plan of the action you would take to class-mates. You might prepare a dramatic monologue that outlines your intentions and perform it for an audience.

For the next scene . . .

Recall a social event you attended or know about which was held to celebrate a happy and important occasion. In what way was the affair organized to acknowledge the special nature of the celebration? Share your recollections with classmates.

Act 4, Scene 1

In this scene . . .

Prospero tells Ferdinand that, after testing him, he is now ready to give Miranda to him in marriage. After warning Ferdinand not to engage in pre-marital sex with Miranda, he asks Ariel to bring forth spirits who will perform a pre-wedding masque (an elaborate form of entertainment in which brightly costumed and masked people perform for an audience). The goddesses Iris, Juno, and Ceres bless the young couple. During the music and dance which follow, Prospero suddenly remembers Caliban's plot to murder him and abruptly ends the celebration.

Caliban, Stephano, and Trinculo arrive. They are soaking wet and reek of the foul odors from the slime-covered pond through which Ariel has lead them. Stephano and Trinculo are distracted by some cheap, gaudy clothes that Ariel has hung on a line as a temptation for them. Caliban urges them to leave the useless clothes, and get on with the murder of Prospero, but the two others ignore his pleas. Then Prospero arrives, ordering his spirits, which are now in the forms of hunting hounds, to chase the three away.

2   *Your compensation makes amends:* Your rewards have made it all worthwhile.

3   *a third . . . life:* one of the most important things in my life

5   *I tender to thy hand:* I give to you; *vexations:* annoyances, difficulties; labours

7   *strangely:* admirably, nobly

9   *boast her off:* tell you things about her that are exaggerations of falsities

10-11   *she will . . . her:* She will prove herself to be far worthier of praise and admiration than any words of mine have suggested.

12   *Against an oracle:* Ferdinand accepts totally Prospero's opinion of his fine daughter. The oracle in Greek society was a priestess who was thought to be the spokesperson of the gods. She provided answers and advice to those who sought help.

15   *virgin-knot:* virginity

18   *aspersion:* blessing

19   *grow:* prosper

23   *As Hymen's . . . you:* as the god of marriage directs you

24   *issue:* children

26   *suggestion:* temptation

27   *Our worser genius:* Satan

Act 4, Scene 1

Before Prospero's cell.

Enter Prospero, Ferdinand, and Miranda.

Prospero: If I have too austerely punish'd you,
  Your compensation makes amends; for I
  Have given you here a third of mine own life,
  Or that for which I live; who once again
  I tender to thy hand: all thy vexations   5
  Were but my trials of thy love, and thou
  Hast strangely stood the test: here, afore Heaven,
  I ratify this my rich gift. O Ferdinand,
  Do not smile at me that I boast her off,
  For thou shalt find she will outstrip all praise,   10
  And make it halt behind her.
Ferdinand: I do believe it
  Against an oracle.
Prospero: Then, as my gift and thine own acquisition
  Worthily purchased, take my daughter: but
  If thou dost break her virgin-knot before   15
  All sanctimonious ceremonies may
  With full and holy rite be minister'd,
  No sweet aspersion shall the heavens let fall
  To make this contract grow; but barren hate,
  Sour-eyed disdain and discord shall bestrew   20
  The union of your bed with weeds so loathly
  That you shall hate it both. Therefore take heed,
  As Hymen's lamps shall light you.
Ferdinand: As I hope
  For quiet days, fair issue and long life,
  With such love as 'tis now, the murkiest den,   25
  The most opportune place, the strong'st suggestion
  Our worser genius can, shall never melt
  Mine honour into lust, to take away

30-31 *Phœbus' steeds . . . below:* Phoebus (or Apollo) was the
sun-god in Greek mythology. Ferdinand says that the
horses which drew Phoebus' chariot across the sky would be
stopped in their travel (and thereby prevent Night from
taking its natural place in the twenty-four hour cycle) before
he would break his vow to consummate his relationship
with Miranda only after it has been blessed through marriage.

37 *the rabble:* the lower spirits at Prospero's service and under
the command of the higher spirit, Ariel

41 *Some vanity of mine art:* some expression or display of my
powers as a magician

43 *with a twink:* in a moment; as quickly as the blinking of an eye

47 *mop and mow:* gestures and appropriate behaviours to the
occasion which they will celebrate

51 *dalliance:* love-making

56 *liver:* The liver was considered to be in man the organ in which
was centred the emotional energies of his being.

57-58 *bring a . . . spirit:* Let us have an over-abundance of spirits to
celebrate the event rather than too few.

Stage direction – *Iris:* the goddess of the rainbow

60 *Ceres:* the goddess of the fields (earth) and keeper of the
harvest which the earth yields

61 *fetches:* beans

The edge of that day's celebration
When I shall think, or Phœbus' steeds are founder'd,   30
Or Night kept chain'd below.
Prospero: Fairly spoke.
Sit, then, and talk with her; she is thine own.
What, Ariel! My industrious servant, Ariel!
[*Enter Ariel.*]
Ariel: What would my potent master? Here I am.
Prospero: Thou and thy meaner fellows your last service   35
Did worthily perform; and I must use you
In such another trick. Go bring the rabble,
O'er whom I give thee power, here to this place:
Incite them to quick motion; for I must
Bestow upon the eyes of this young couple   40
Some vanity of mine art: it is my promise,
And they expect it from me.
Ariel: Presently?
Prospero: Ay, with a twink.
Ariel: Before you can say "come" and "go",
And breathe twice and cry "so, so",   45
Each one, tripping on his toe,
Will be here with mop and mow.
Do you love me, master? No?
Prospero: Dearly, my delicate Ariel. Do not approach
Till thou dost hear me call.
Ariel: Well, I conceive.   [*Exit.*] 50
Prospero: Look thou be true; do not give dalliance
Too much the rein. The strongest oaths are straw
To the fire i' the blood. Be more abstemious,
Or else, good night to your vow!
Ferdinand: I warrant you, sir;
The white cold virgin snow upon my heart   55
Abates the ardour of my liver.
Prospero: Well.
Now come, my Ariel! Bring a corollary,
Rather than want a spirit: appear, and pertly!
No tongue! All eyes! Be silent.   [*Soft music.*]
[*Enter Iris.*]
Iris: Ceres, most bounteous lady, thy rich leas   60
Of wheat, rye, barley, fetches, oats and pease;

63   *thatch'd with stover:* covered with grass for sheep to graze upon

64   *with pioned and twilled brims:* The banks of the rivers covered with peonies, marsh marigolds, and reeds.

65   *at thy hest betrims:* At thy command, nature becomes beautiful.

66   *To make . . . crowns:* to make for young maidens, not yet in love, beautiful floral ornaments to wear as ornament and jewellery

66-67   *broom-groves/Whose . . . loves:* the brown, lifeless bushes not yet warmed by the Spring sun and into which the rejected young lover escapes to find comfort in his misery.

68   *pole-clipt vineyard:* grape vines which have been clipped in such a way to ensure they grow evenly around the poles to which they are attached

70   *Where thou thyself dost air:* where you rest to enjoy the fresh air; *the queen o' the sky:* Juno

74   *her peacocks fly amain:* Peacocks were the birds who drew Juno's chariot.

78   *saffron:* a plant with deep orange-coloured flowers

81   *bosky:* covered with trees and bushes; *unshrubb'd down:* hills without shrubs or bushes

82   *Rich scarf . . . earth:* a completion of the description of the rainbow begun in line 78. This is the way it appears to its viewers upon the earth's surface.

85   *And some . . . estate:* and to give to the young lovers some present to commemorate this special occasion

87   *Venus or her son:* Venus the goddess of love and her son, Cupid

89   *dusky Dis:* a reference to Pluto ("Dis") the god of the underworld. In mythology, he abducted Proserpina the daughter of Ceres.

93   *Paphos:* a town in Cyprus which is sacred to the worship of Venus

94   *Dove-drawn:* Doves drew Venus' chariot on her travels through the heavens.

97   *Hymen's torch be lighted:* The god of marriage, Hymen, guided the couple to their marriage bed with his light.

Thy turfy mountains, where live nibbling sheep,
And flat meads thatch'd with stover, them to keep;
Thy banks with pioned and twilled brims,
Which spongy April at thy hest betrims,   65
To make cold nymphs chaste crowns; and thy broom-
    groves,
Whose shadow the dismissed bachelor loves,
Being lass-lorn; thy pole-clipt vineyard;
And thy sea-marge, sterile and rocky hard,
Where thou thyself dost air;—the queen o' the sky,   70
Whose watery arch and messenger am I,
Bids thee leave these, and with her sovereign grace,
Here on this grass-plot, in this very place,
To come and sport:—her peacocks fly amain:
Approach rich Ceres, her to entertain.   75
[*Enter Ceres.*]
Ceres: Hail, many-colour'd messenger, that ne'er
Dost disobey the wife of Jupiter;
Who, with thy saffron wings, upon my flowers
Diffusest honey-drops, refreshing showers;
And with each end of thy blue bow dost crown   80
My bosky acres and my unshrubb'd down,
Rich scarf to my proud earth;—why hath thy queen
Summon'd me hither, to this short-grass'd green?
Iris: A contract of true love to celebrate;
And some donation freely to estate   85
On the blest lovers.
Ceres: Tell me, heavenly bow,
If Venus or her son, as thou dost know,
Do now attend the queen? Since they did plot
The means that dusky Dis my daughter got,
Her and her blind boy's scandal'd company   90
I have forsworn.
Iris: Of her society
Be not afraid: I met her deity
Cutting the clouds towards Paphos, and her son
Dove-drawn with her. Here thought they to have done
Some wanton charm upon this man and maid,   95
Whose vows are, that no bed-right shall be paid
Till Hymen's torch be lighted: but in vain;

98   *hot minion:* Venus, the energetic, hot-blooded mistress of Mars

99   *waspish-headed:* refers to Cupid's hot temper

102   *Juno:* Queen of the gods; *her gait:* her majestic bearing

104   *twain:* couple

105   *their issue:* their children

110   *foison:* abundance

113   *burthen:* burden, referring here to the abundance of fruit upon the plants

114-115 *Spring come . . . harvest:* This is Ceres' wish for the young couple that they may have no winter, but that after harvest (autumn) spring may come.

119   *Harmonious charmingly:* a reference to the magic and music by which the sights were conjured

120-121 *Spirits, which . . . confines:* Prospero speaks of the lower spirits whom he has called forth from the places in which they are imprisoned until such times they are allowed to walk on earth.

128   *windering:* winding, or perhaps, wandering

129   *sedged crowns:* crowns made of coarse grass that grow along the banks of streams

130   *crisp channels:* the winding courses through which the streams flow

Mar's hot minion is return'd again;
Her waspish-headed son has broke his arrows,
Swears he will shoot no more but play with sparrows,   100
And be a boy right out.
Ceres: High'st queen of state,
Great Juno comes; I know her by her gait.
[*Enter Juno.*]
Juno: How does my bounteous sister? Go with me
To bless this twain, that they may prosperous be
And honour'd in their issue.   [*They sing.*] 105
Juno: *Honour, riches, marriage-blessing,*
             Long continuance, and increasing,
             Hourly joys be still upon you!
             Juno sings her blessings on you.
Ceres: *Earth's increase, foison plenty,*   110
             Barns and garners never empty;
             Vines with clustering bunches growing;
             Plants with goodly burthen bowing;
             Spring come to you at the farthest
             In the very end of harvest!   115
             Scarcity and want shall shun you;
             Ceres' blessing so is on you.
Ferdinand: This is a most majestic vision, and
Harmonious charmingly. May I be bold
To think these spirits?
Prospero: Spirits, which by mine art   120
I have from their confines call'd to enact
My present fancies.
Ferdinand: Let me live here ever;
So rare a wonder'd father and a wife
Makes this place Paradise.
[*Juno and Ceres whisper, and send Iris on employment.*]
Prospero: Sweet, now, silence!
Juno and Ceres whisper seriously;   125
There's something else to do: hush, and be mute,
Or else our spell is marr'd.
Iris: You nymphs, call'd Naiads, of the windering brooks,
With your sedged crowns and ever-harmless looks,
Leave your crisp channels and on this green land   130
Answer your summons; Juno does command:

Come, temperate nymphs, and help to celebrate
A contract of true love; be not too late.
Enter certain Nymphs.
You sunburnt sicklemen, of August weary,
Come hither from the furrow and be merry: 135
Make holiday: your rye-straw hats put on,
And these fresh nymphs encounter every one
In country footing.
[*Enter certain Reapers, properly habited: they join with the*
    Nymphs in a graceful dance; towards the end whereof
    Prospero starts suddenly, and speaks; after which to a
    strange, hollow, and confused noise, they heavily vanish.]
Prospero: [*Aside.*] I had forgot that foul conspiracy
Of the beast Caliban and his confederates   140
Against my life: the minute of their plot
Is almost come. [*To the Spirits.*] Well done! avoid; no
    more!
Ferdinand: This strange: your father's in some passion
That works him strongly.
Miranda: Never till this day
Saw I him touch'd with anger so distemper'd.   145
Prospero: You do look, my son, in a moved sort,
As if you were dismay'd: be cheerful, sir.
Our revels now are ended. These our actors,
As I foretold you, were all spirits, and
Are melted into air, into thin air: 150
And, like the baseless fabric of this vision,
The cloud-capp'd towers, the gorgeous palaces,
The solemn temples, the great globe itself,
Yea, all which it inherit, shall dissolve,
And, like this insubstantial pageant faded,   155
Leave not a rack behind. We are such stuff
As dreams are made on; and our little life
Is rounded with a sleep. Sir, I am vex'd;
Bear with my weakness; my old brain is troubled:
Be not disturb'd with my infirmity: 160
If you be pleased, retire into my cell,
And there repose: a turn or two I'll walk,
To still my beating mind.
Ferdinand, Miranda: We wish your peace. [*Exeunt.*]

164   *with a thought:* as quickly as a thought

165   *cleave to:* grasp and hold onto until I carry out your orders

170   *varlets:* rascals

174   *bending:* moving in the direction towards

176   *unback'd:* unridden; not yet broken into the saddle

177   *Advanced:* lifted up

179   *lowing:* music

180   *goss:* thick and spiny shrubs

182   *filthy-mantled pool:* The pool was covered with a green scrum; stagnant

186   *trumpery:* worthless but gaudy (flashy) clothing

187   *stale:* A strap. A "stale" was a stuffed bird used as a decoy in hunting game birds.

188-189 *on whose . . . stick:* Prospero believes at this point that no amount of care, kindness or training can ever raise Caliban above the level of the vile condition of his past and present state.

192   *cankers:* an ulcerous sore that appears inside the mouth or on the lips

Prospero: Come with a thought. I thank thee, Ariel: come.
   [*Enter Ariel.*]
Ariel: Thy thoughts I cleave to. What's thy pleasure?
Prospero: Spirit, 165
  We must prepare to meet with Caliban.
Ariel: Ay, my commander: when I presented Ceres,
  I thought to have told thee of it; but I fear'd
  Lest I might anger thee.
Prospero: Say again, where didst thou leave these varlets?   170
Ariel: I told you, sir, they were red-hot with drinking;
  So full of valour that they smote the air
  For breathing in their faces; beat the ground
  For kissing of their feet; yet always bending
  Towards their project. Then I beat my tabor;   175
  At which, like unback'd colts, they prick'd their ears,
  Advanced their eyelids, lifted up their noses
  As they smelt music: so I charm'd their ears,
  That calf-like they my lowing followed through
  Tooth'd briers, sharp furzes, pricking goss, and thorns,   180
  Which enter'd their frail shins: at last I left them
  I' the filthy-mantled pool beyond your cell,
  There dancing up to the chins, that the foul lake
  O'erstunk their feet.
Prospero: This was well done, my bird.
  Thy shape invisible retain thou still: 185
  The trumpery in my house, go bring it hither,
  For stale to catch these thieves.
Ariel: I go, I go.   [*Exit.*]
Prospero: A devil, a born devil, on whose nature
  Nurture can never stick; on whom my pains,
  Humanely taken, all, all lost, quite lost;   190
  And as with age his body uglier grows,
  So his mind cankers. I will plague them all,
  Even to roaring.
  [*Re-enter Ariel, loaden with glistening apparel, etc.*]
                Come, hang them on this line.
  [*Prospero and Ariel remain, invisible. Enter Caliban,*
    Stephano, and Trinculo, all wet.]
Caliban: Pray you, tread softly, that the blind mole may
  not

197   *played the Jack:* a reference to the jack-o'-lantern, who like the will-o'-the-wisp lead people into danger

206   *Shall hoodwink this mischance:* shall cause this accident to be forgotten. In other words, Caliban continues to promise Stephano the prize which they both planned to take (to "hoodwink" means to deceive or trick)

213   *o'er ears:* over my ears in water

216   *mouth o' the cell:* the entrance way to Prospero's dwelling

217   *good mischief:* evil towards Prospero but good or advantageous for themselves, the conspirators

226   *frippery:* an old-clothes shop. Trinculo points out to Caliban that as butler and jester, they are good judges of cast-off or second-hand clothes.

231   *To dote . . . luggage:* to desire so foolishly such useless clothes

234   *Make us strange stuff:* Prospero will work some painful charm upon them.

Hear a foot fall: we now are near his cell.   195
Stephano: Monster, your fairy, which you say is a harmless
    fairy, has done little better than played the Jack with
    us.
Trinculo: Monster, I do smell all horse-piss, at which my
    nose is in great indignation.   200
Stephano: So is mine. Do you hear, monster? If I should
    take a displeasure against you, look you,—
Trinculo: Thou wert but a lost monster.
Caliban: Good, my lord, give me thy favour still.
    Be patient, for the prize I'll bring thee to   205
    Shall hoodwink this mischance: therefore speak softly.
    All's hush'd as midnight yet.
Trinculo: Ay, but to lose our bottles in the pool,—
Stephano: There is not only disgrace and dishonour in that,
    monster, but an infinite loss.   210
Trinculo: That's more to me than my wetting: yet this is
    your harmless fairy, monster.
Stephano: I will fetch off my bottle, though I be o'er ears
    for my labour.
Caliban: Prithee, my king, be quiet. See'st thou here,   215
    This is the mouth o' the cell: no noise, and enter.
    Do that good mischief which may make this island
    Thine own for ever, and I, thy Caliban,
    For aye thy foot-licker.
Stephano: Give me thy hand. I do begin to have bloody   220
    thoughts.
Trinculo: O king Stephano! O peer! O worthy Stephano!
    look what a wardrobe here is for thee!
Caliban: Let it alone, thou fool; it is but trash.
Trinculo: O, ho, monster! We know what belongs to a   225
    frippery. O king Stephano!
Stephano: Put off that gown, Trinculo; by this hand I'll have
    that gown.
Trinculo: Thy Grace shall have it.
Caliban: The dropsy drown this fool! What do you mean   230
    To dote thus on such luggage? Let's along
    And do the murder first: if he awake,
    From toe to crown he'll fill our skins with pinches,
    Make us strange stuff.

236   *jerkin?:* a doublet, i.e., a close-fitting jacket worn by men in the 16th and 17th centuries

237   *lose your hair:* With this expression, Stephano attempts a pun on the word "line," line 236. One meaning of the word is obviously a clothes-line which was often made of hair. A second meaning of the word is "equator." Stephano speaks of losing hair in reference to the sailors who, when travelling below the equator, often contracted a fever which resulted in hair loss.

239   *by line and level:* according to rule (another pun on the world "line" which refers to the plumb line and carpenter's level). The plumb line is used to measure verticality or depth; *an't like:* if it please

243-244 *pass/of pate:* a joke; a "pass" here is a sword thrust; "pate" is another word for head.

245   *lime:* bird lime, a sticky substance placed on twigs to trap birds; here it suggests a thief who is often referred to as having sticky fingers

259   *dry convulsions:* violent contractions of the muscles causing great pain in the joints

260   *aged cramps:* the sort of cramps that come with old age

261   *pard or cat o' mountain:* leopard or mountain cat

Stephano: Be you quiet, monster. Mistress line, is not this   235
    my jerkin? Now is the jerkin under the line: now, jer-
    kin, you are like to lose your hair, and prove a bald
    jerkin.
Trinculo: Do, do: we steal by line and level, an't like your
    Grace.   240
Stephano: I thank thee for that jest; here's a garment for't:
    wit shall not go unrewarded while I am king of this
    country. "Steal by line and level" is an excellent pass
    of pate; there's another garment for't.
Trinculo: Monster, come, put some lime upon your fingers,   245
    and away with the rest.
Caliban: I will have none on't: we shall lose our time,
    And all be turn'd to barnacles, or to apes
    With foreheads villainous low.
Stephano: Monster, lay to your fingers: help to bear this   250
    away where my hogshead of wine is, or I'll turn you
    out of my kingdom: go to, carry this.
Trinculo: And this.
Stephano: Ay, and this.
    [*A noise of hunters heard. Enter divers Spirits, in shape of*
    dogs and hounds, hunting them about; Prospero and Ariel
    setting them on.]
Prospero: Hey, Mountain, hey!   255
Ariel: Silver! There it goes, Silver!
Prospero: Fury, Fury! There, Tyrant, there! Hark! Hark!
        [*Caliban, Stephano, and Trinculo are driven out.*]
    Go charge my goblins that they grind their joints
    With dry convulsions; shorten up their sinews
    With aged cramps; and more pinch-spotted make them   260
    Than pard or cat o' mountain.
Ariel: Hark, they roar!
Prospero: Let them be hunted soundly. At this hour
    Lies at my mercy all mine enemies;
    Shortly shall all my labours end, and thou
    Shalt have the air at freedom: for a little   265
    Follow, and do me service.   [*Exeunt.*]

Act 4: Consider the Whole Act

1. Examine Prospero's first two speeches in this act. What does he say to Ferdinand about Miranda? Do you think his feelings are representative of the way most parents feel about their children? Record your thoughts in a journal entry.

2. In a small group research the topic of the masque as a form of entertainment. Summarize your findings and share them with other groups. Why do you think Shakespeare chose to include a masque in this play?

3. Iris, Ceres, and Juno appear as representatives of the Greek deities during the masque. Investigate the position, roles, and responsibilities of each of these characters as they are described in mythology.

   Prepare and present a report, explaining the appropriateness of their presence at this masque. In your report, you might suggest other suitable deities for inclusion at this occasion.

4. Prospero's speech in lines 146–163 is one of the most famous ones in the play. In a journal entry, write the ideas he expresses in your own words. In what way does his comment that "we are such stuff as dreams are made on" correspond or conflict with your ideas about life? Share your reactions and opinions with a partner.

5. As Prospero, compose a personal journal entry in which you write about the emotional extremes you have experienced during the events of Act 4. Explain why the foolish and impossible attempts of Caliban to murder you and take over control of your island have so angered you. Compare and discuss your explanation with those of your classmates.

6. In a group, stage your own masque that includes dance, music, and goddesses. Before you begin consider the following questions:
   - Who will the characters be and what or whom will they represent?
   - What costumes, props, make-up, lighting, music, and special effects will you use?
   - How will your performers move?

   Rehearse and then perform your masque for the class.

7. This act juxtaposes two elements:
   - true love celebrated by goddesses, nymphs, and reapers,
   - foolish ambition pursued by three drunks.

   In your group discuss these contrasting elements. Select key lines and events that illustrate these contradictory elements of this act. Examine the lines of the text that bridge the two sections. Do the two episodes have any common features? Explain your ideas to your classmates and invite their responses.

For the next scene . . .

Imagine you were to be reunited with a friend or relative from a far-away place. Many years have passed since you communicated last with this person. How do you think you would feel? How might you spend the first few hours or days together? What questions might you ask? What important aspects of your life would you want to talk about? Do you think the relationship you had with the person will be the same as it once was? Record your ideas in a journal entry.

Act 5, Scene 1

In this scene . . .

Dressed in his magic robes Prospero announces to Ariel that his plan is nearing completion. He asks about Alonso, Antonio, Sebastian, and Gonzalo. Ariel suggests that Prospero take pity on them. Prospero sends Ariel to bring them before him so he can restore them to their senses. In a soliloquy, he declares that he will give up his magic. Ariel returns, leading the royal party into the charmed circle that Prospero has drawn on the ground with his staff. Prospero speaks to the four while each is still spellbound. Then, before they awake, he takes off his magic robes and puts on the clothes he wore when he was the Duke of Milan. As the men are released from the spell, Prospero begins to explain something of what has been happening, including what has occurred between Ferdinand and Miranda. Ariel then brings in the ship's Master and Boatswain who declare that the ship is in perfect condition. Finally, Caliban, Stephano, and Trinculo, still dressed in their stolen apparel are brought in, reprimanded, and set off to prepare Prospero's cell. Prospero then invites everyone into the cell where he will relate to them his life and, in particular, the details of his years in exile on the island. In his final command to Ariel, Prospero asks him to make certain that tomorrow brings perfect sailing conditions for the return journey to Naples. He then bids farewell to Ariel and frees him from his service.

In the Epilogue, Prospero addresses the audience. He begs that he, too, will be allowed to return home. He acknowledges that, without magic, he must rely on prayer and mercy.

1   *gather to a head:* nears its completion

2   *crack not:* don't weaken; remain impatient

2-3   *time/Goes . . . carriage:* Literally, time is personified as a man walking straight and towards his intended destination. In other words, Prospero's project is working out in accordance with his plan.

7   *How fares:* how are

10   *In the . . . cell:* in the grove of linden trees which shields your cell (home) from the winds of sea and storms

11   *till your release:* until you (Prospero) release them from the spell which holds them

12   *abide all three distracted:* Sebastian, Antonio, and Alonso remain still in their fit of madness.

17   *eaves of reeds:* the eaves of a roof projecting beyond the walls. Reeds were used to thatch the roof of a house of building.

24   *be kindlier moved:* be even more forgiving – as a human with a greater capacity for strong feelings than you a spirit creature of the air.

25   *Though with . . . quick:* Although, by their great crimes I have been hurt to the very core.

Act 5, Scene 1

Before Prospero's cell.

*Enter Prospero in his magic robes,
and Ariel.*

Prospero: Now does my project gather to a head:
My charms crack not; my spirits obey; and time
Goes upright with his carriage. How's the day?
Ariel: On the sixth hour; at which time, my lord
You said our work should cease.
Prospero: I did say so, 5
When first I raised the tempest. Say, my spirit,
How fares the king and's followers?
Ariel: Confined together
In the same fashion as you gave in charge,
Just as you left them; all prisoners, sir,
In the line-grove which weather-fends your cell; 10
They cannot budge till your release. The king,
His brother, and yours, abide all three distracted,
And the remainder mourning over them,
Brimful of sorrow and dismay; but chiefly
Him that you term'd, sir, "The good old lord, Gonzalo"; 15
His tears run down his beard, like winter's drops
From eaves of reeds. Your charm so strongly works 'em,
That if you now beheld them, your affections
Would become tender.
Prospero: Dost thou think so, spirit?
Ariel: Mine would, sir, were I human.
Prospero: And mine shall. 20
Hast thou, which art but air, a touch, a feeling
Of their afflictions, and shall not myself,
One of their kind, that relish all as sharply,
Passion as they, be kindlier moved than thou art?
Though with their high wrongs I am struck to the quick, 25
Yet with my nobler reason 'gainst my fury

29   *sole drift:* only intention

35   *ebbing Neptune:* the outgoing tide

36   *demi-puppets:* fairies of a diminutive size

37   *By moonshine . . . make:* in the moonlight make rings of some grass. Such circles of rank grass were believed to be formed by the dancing of fairies. The phenomenon is now known to be caused by the effect of the underground part of the toadstool on grass roots.

39   *to make midnight mushrooms;* Mushrooms grow over night. It was believed that they were produced by elves at the midnight hour.

40   *the solemn curfew:* spirts who rejoice to hear night's curfew because it frees them from their confines to walk upon the earth until the cock crows at dawn

41   *Weak masters:* although your powers may be small

43   *azured vault:* the blue sky

46   *promontory:* a high ridge of land or rock jutting out into a sea or other body of water

49   *oped:* opened

51   *abjure:* give up

59   *unsettled fancy:* a troubled or tormented mind

I rather let them go than take vengeance which isn't normal

Do I take part: the rarer action is
In virtue than in vengeance: they being penitent,
The sole drift of my purpose doth extend
Not a frown further. Go release them, Ariel: 30
My charms I'll break, their senses I'll restore,
And they shall be themselves.
Ariel: I'll fetch them, sir. [*Exit.*]
Prospero: Ye elves of hills, brooks, standing lakes, and
    groves;
And ye that on the sands with printless foot
Do chase the ebbing Neptune, and do fly him   35
When he comes back; you demi-puppets that
By moonshine do the green sour ringlets make,
Whereof the ewe not bites; and you whose pastime
Is to make midnight mushrooms, that rejoice
To hear the solemn curfew; by whose aid,—   40
Weak masters though ye be,—I have bedimm'd
The noontide sun, call'd forth the mutinous winds,
And 'twixt the green sea and the azured vault
Set roaring war: to the dread rattling thunder
Have I given fire, and rifted Jove's stout oak   45
With his own bolt; the strong-based promontory
Have I made shake, and by the spurs pluck'd up
The pine and cedar: graves at my command
Have waked their sleepers, oped, and let 'em forth
By my so potent art. But this rough magic   50
I here abjure; and, when I have required
Some heavenly music,—which even now I do,—
To work mine end upon their senses, that
This airy charm is for, I'll break my staff,
Bury it certain fathoms in the earth,   55
And deeper than did ever plummet sound
I'll drown my book.   [*Solemn music.*]
[*Re-enter Ariel before: then Alonso, with a frantic gesture,
    attended by Gonzalo; Sebastian and Antonio in like
    manner, attended by Adrian and Francisco: they all enter
    the circle which Prospero had made, and there stand
    charmed; which Prospero observing, speaks:*]
A solemn air, and the best comforter
To an unsettled fancy, cure thy brains,

63-64   *Mine eyes . . . drops:* I also weep in sympathy with you.

64   *apace:* quickly

73   *furtherer:* accessory, helper

76   *Expell'd remorse and nature:* cast out of your soul all pity and
        brotherly feeling

79-82   *Their understanding/ . . . muddy:* The flood of their returning
        reason will soon overpower the disorder in their minds.

85   *discase:* disrobe

86   *Milan:* Duke of Milan

90   *couch:* lie

92   *After summer:* in chase of summer

96   *so, so, so:* Prospero responds to Ariel's expression of delight
        in considering the freedom Ariel will soon have.

Now useless, boil'd within thy skull! There stand, 60
For you are spell-stopp'd.
Holy Gonzalo, honourable man,
Mine eyes, even sociable to the show of thine,
Fall fellowly drops. The charm dissolves apace;
And as the morning steals upon the night, 65
Melting the darkness, so their rising senses
Begin to chase the ignorant fumes that mantle
Their clearer reason. O good Gonzalo,
My true preserver, and a loyal sir
To him thou follow'st! I will pay thy graces 70
Home both in word and deed. Most cruelly
Didst thou, Alonso, use me and my daughter:
Thy brother was a furtherer in the act.
Thou art pinch'd for't now, Sebastian. Flesh and blood,
You, brother mine, that entertain'd ambition, 75
Expell'd remorse and nature; who, with Sebastian,—
Whose inward pinches therefore are most strong,—
Would here have kill'd your king; I do forgive thee,
Unnatural though thou art. Their understanding
Begins to swell; and the approaching tide 80
Will shortly fill the reasonable shore,
That now lies foul and muddy. Not one of them
That yet looks on me, or would know me: Ariel,
Fetch me the hat and rapier in my cell:
I will discase me, and myself present 85
As I was sometime Milan: quickly, spirit;
Thou shalt ere long be free.
Ariel: [*Sings and helps to attire him.*]
    Where the bee sucks, there lurk I:
    In a cowslip's bell I lie;
    There I couch when owls do cry. 90
    On the bat's back I do fly
    After summer merrily.
   Merrily, merrily shall I live now
   Under the blossom that hangs on the bough.
Prospero: Why, that's my dainty Ariel! I shall miss thee; 95
But yet thou shalt have freedom: so, so, so.
To the king's ship, invisible as thou art:
There shalt thou find the mariners asleep

99   *Under the hatches:* Hatches are wooden coverings for the openings on a ship's deck. It is to the undersection of these hatches that the mariners were fastened after the tempest.

103   *Or e'er:* before

112   *enchanted trifle to abuse me:* unreal (illusory) magical appearance to deceive my sight and reason

116-117 *this must . . . story:* This appearance (of Prospero) granting that it is real must be accounted for by a strange and wonderful story.

124   *subtilties:* enchantments, deceptions

127   *pluck his Highness' frown:* direct King Alonso's anger towards you

128   *justify:* prove, show conclusively

Under the hatches; the master and the boatswain
Being awake, enforce them to this place,   100
And presently, I prithee.
Ariel: I drink the air before me, and return
Or e'er your pulse twice beat.   [*Exit.*]
Gonzalo: All torment, trouble, wonder and amazement
Inhabits here: some heavenly power guide us   105
Out of this fearful country! *Always good from bad*
Prospero: Behold, sir king,
The wronged Duke of Milan, Prospero:
For more assurance that a living prince
Does now speak to thee, I embrace thy body;
And to thee and thy company I bid   110
A hearty welcome.
Alonso: Whether thou be'st he or no,
Or some enchanted trifle to abuse me,
As late I have been, I not know: thy pulse
Beats as of flesh and blood; and, since I saw thee,
The affliction of my mind amends, with which,   115
I fear, a madness held me: this must crave,—
An if this be at all—a most strange story.
Thy dukedom I resign, and do entreat
Thou pardon me my wrongs.—But how should Prospero
Be living and be here?
Prospero: First, noble friend,   120
Let me embrace thine age, whose honour cannot
Be measured or confined.
Gonzalo: Whether this be
Or be not, I'll not swear.
Prospero: You do yet taste
Some subtilties o' the isle, that will not let you
Believe things certain. Welcome, my friends all!   125
[*Aside to Sebastian and Antonio.*]
But you, my brace of lords, were I so minded,
I here could pluck his Highness' frown upon you
And justify you traitors: at this time
I will tell no tales.
Sebastian: [*Aside.*]   The devil speaks in him.
Prospero: No.
For you, most wicked sir, whom to call brother   130

132   *rankest:* worst, foulest

133   *perforce:* by force, by compulsion

139   *woe for't:* sorry for it

140-141 *patience/Says . . . cure:* patience (spoken of as a female deity throughout lines 140-143) has no remedy for my loss

142   *her:* patience's; *soft grace:* soothing or comforting nature

143   *sovereign aid:* all-powerful help or comfort

145   *As great . . . late:* as great to me as your loss and as recent

145-146 *supportable/To . . . loss:* and to help me endure such great loss

146   *much weaker:* Perhaps Prospero is reminding Alonso that he has at least another child, Claribel, to comfort him if Ferdinand is lost, while he (Prospero) has only one child. Hence, he has less comfort to support him in the loss of a child. (Prospero is simply taunting Alonso at this point.)

151   *mudded:* buried

154-155 *At this . . . reason:* At this meeting it is apparent that these lords (Sebastian and Antonio) are so amazed that they can't believe it; *devour their reason:* distrust their reason

155-156 *scarce think/ . . . truth:* They can't believe their eyes.

158   *justled:* jostled; *justled from your senses:* made mad

163   *'tis a . . . day:* It is a story to be told over a period of time; it can't be told in only a day.

Would even infect my mouth, I do forgive
Thy rankest fault,—all of them; and require
My dukedom of thee, which perforce I know,
Thou must restore.

Alonso: If thou be'st Prospero,
    Give us particulars of thy preservation;   135
    How thou hast met us here, who three hours since
    Were wreck'd upon this shore; where I have lost—
    How sharp the point of this remembrance is!—
    My dear son Ferdinand.

Prospero: I am woe for't, sir.

Alonso: Irreparable is the loss, and patience   140
    Says it is past her cure.

Prospero: I rather think
    You have not sought her help, of whose soft grace
    For the like loss I have her sovereign aid,
    And rest myself content.

Alonso: You the like loss!

Prospero: As great to me as late; and supportable   145
    To make the dear loss, have I means much weaker
    Than you may call to comfort you, for I
    Have lost my daughter.

Alonso: A daughter?
    O heavens, that they were living both in Naples,
    The king and queen there! That they were, I wish   150
    Myself were mudded in that oozy bed
    Where my son lies. When did you lose your daughter?

Prospero: In this last tempest. I perceive, these lords
    At this encounter do so much admire,
    That they devour their reason, and scarce think   155
    Their eyes do offices of truth, their words
    Are natural breath: but, howsoe'er you have
    Been justled from your senses, know for certain
    That I am Prospero, and that very duke
    Which was thrust forth of Milan; who most strangely   160
    Upon this shore, where you were wreck'd, was landed,
    To be the lord on't. No more yet of this;
    For 'tis a chronicle of day by day,
    Not a relation for a breakfast, nor
    Befitting this first meeting. Welcome, sir;   165

169   *requite:* reciprocate

172   *play me false:* You're not playing fairly.

174-175 *Yes, for . . . play:* Even if you were to try to cheat me out of twenty kingdoms, I love you so much I would still call it fair play.

175-176 *If this . . . island:* if what I behold is but another magical illusion like the others we have seen on this island

186   *eld'st:* longest

187   *sever'd:* separated

This cell's my court: here have I few attendants,
And subjects none abroad: pray you, look in.
My dukedom since you have given me again,
I will requite you with as good a thing;
At least bring forth a wonder, to content ye   170
As much as me my dukedom.
[*Here Prospero discovers Ferdinand and Miranda playing
    at chess.*]
Miranda: Sweet lord, you play me false.
Ferdinand: No, my dear'st
    love,
I would not for the world.
Miranda: Yes, for a score of kingdoms you should wrangle,
And I would call it fair play.
Alonso: If this prove   175
A vision of the island, one dear son
Shall I twice lose.
Sebastian: A most high miracle!
Ferdinand: Though the seas threaten, they are merciful;
I have cursed them without cause.   [*Kneels.*]
Alonso: Now all the blessings
Of a glad father compass thee about!   180
Arise, and say how thou camest here.
Miranda: O, wonder!
How many goodly creatures are there here!
How beauteous mankind is! O brave new world,
That has such people in't!
Prospero: 'Tis new to thee.
Alonso: What is this maid with whom thou wast at play?   185
Your eld'st acquaintance cannot be three hours:
Is she the goddess that hath sever'd us,
And brought us thus together?
Ferdinand: Sir, she is mortal;
But by immortal Providence she's mine:
I chose her when I could not ask my father   190
For his advice, nor thought I had one. She
Is daughter to this famous Duke of Milan,
Of whom so often I have heard renown,
But never saw before; of whom I have
Received a second life; and second father   195

196   *I am hers:* I am her father, too.

199-200 *Let us . . . gone:* Let us not burden ourselves with memories
        of sorrows that are now past.

203   *chalk'd forth:* marked out

207-208 *set it . . . pillars:* Gonzalo suggested that the story of this joyous
        occasion should be inscribed in gold upon lasting pillows.

213   *When no . . . own:* Gonzalo is referring to the strange madness
        which had held King Alonso and his companions captive.

214   *still embrace his heart:* ever he his fate

218-219 *Now, blasphemy/ . . . shore:* Unlike the time you were at sea
        and blasphemed (cursed) enough to cause God's grace
        to be withdrawn from us, do not utter any blasphemy (curse
        against God) on shore.

220   *Hast thou . . . land?:* Can you not speak when you are on land?
        He remembers that the boatswain was very vocal while on
        the ship during the tempest.

223   *three glasses since:* three hours ago; *gave our split:* believed
        to be wrecked

224   *tight and yare:* sound and ready, i.e., seaworthy

This lady makes him to me.
Alonso: I am hers:
But, O, how oddly will it sound that I
Must ask my child forgiveness!
Prospero: There, sir, stop:
Let us not burthen our remembrance with
A heaviness that's gone.
Gonzalo: I have inly wept,   200
Or should have spoke ere this. Look down, you gods
And on this couple drop a blessed crown!
For it is you that have chalk'd forth the way
Which brought us hither.
Alonso: I say Amen, Gonzalo!
Gonzalo: Was Milan thrust from Milan, that his issue   205
Should become kings of Naples? O, rejoice
Beyond a common joy! And set it down
With gold on lasting pillars. In one voyage
Did Claribel her husband find at Tunis,
And Ferdinand, her brother, found a wife   210
Where he himself was lost, Prospero his dukedom
In a poor isle, and all of us ourselves
When no man was his own.
Alonso: [*To Ferdinand and Miranda.*] Give me your hands:
Let grief and sorrow still embrace his heart
That doth not wish you joy!
Gonzalo: Be it so! Amen!   215
[*Re-enter Ariel, with the Master and Boatswain amazedly
     following.*]
O look, sir, look, sir! Here is more of us:
I prophesied, if a gallows were on land,
This fellow could not drown. Now, blasphemy,
That swear'st grace o'erboard, not an oath on shore?
Hast thou no mouth by land? What is the news?   220
Boatswain: The best news is, that we have safely found
Our king and company; the next, our ship—
Which, but three glasses since, we gave out split—
Is tight and yare and bravely rigg'd, as when
We first put out to sea.
Ariel: [*Aside to Prospero.*] Sir, all this service   225
Have I done since I went.

226   *tricksy:* clever

227-228 *they strengthen/ . . . stranger:* These events become stranger
        and stranger to our understanding.

238   *Capering to eye her:* dancing with joy to behold the ship so
        seaworthy

240   *moping:* in a daze

242   *trod:* travelled

243-244 *more than . . . of:* more than has ever happened as a result of
        natural causes (he implies that it must have been the result
        of magical causes)

244-245 *some oracle/ . . . knowledge:* Only some higher power can
        explain these strange events to us.

247-250 *at pick'd . . . accidents:* Prospero promises here to explain
        all the events that have happened and that still remain
        mysterious to the King and his party.

256-257 *let no . . . himself:* Stephano is apparently still strongly under
        the influence of the liquor he has drunk in such large
        quantity. He inverts the expression: every man for himself.

257   *Coragio:* courage

Prospero: [*Aside to Ariel.*]   My tricksy spirit!
Alonso: These are not natural events; they strengthen
    From strange to stranger. Say, how came you hither?
Boatswain: If I did think, sir, I were well awake,
    I'd strive to tell you. We were dead of sleep,   230
    And—how we know not—all clapp'd under hatches;
    Where but even now, with strange and several noises
    Of roaring, shrieking, howling, jingling chains,
    And mo diversity of sounds, all horrible,
    We were awaked; straightway, at liberty;   235
    Where we, in all her trim, freshly beheld
    Our royal, good and gallant ship; our master
    Capering to eye her:—on a trice, so please you,
    Even in a dream, were we divided from them,
    And were brought moping hither.
Ariel: [*Aside to Prospero.*]   Was't well done?   240
Prospero: [*Aside to Ariel.*] Bravely, my diligence. Thou shalt
    be free.
Alonso: This is as strange a maze as e'er men trod;
    And there is in this business more than nature
    Was ever conduct of: some oracle
    Must rectify our knowledge.
Prospero: Sir, my liege,   245
    Do not infest your mind with beating on
    The strangeness of this business; at pick'd leisure,
    Which shall be shortly, single I'll resolve you,
    Which to you shall seem probable, of every
    These happen'd accidents; till when, be cheerful   250
    And think of each thing well. [*Aside to Ariel.*] Come
    hither, spirit:
    Set Caliban and his companions free;
    Untie the spell. [*Exit Ariel.*] How fares my gracious sir?
    There are yet missing of your company
    Some few odd lads that you remember not.   255
    [*Re-enter Ariel, driving in Caliban, Stephano, and Trinculo,*
    in their stolen apparel.]
Stephano: Every man shift for all the rest, and let no man
    take care for himself; for all is but fortune.—Coragio,
    bully-monster, coragio!

259   *spies:* eyes

261   *brave spirits:* fine-looking spirits

266   *Is a plain fish:* is obviously a fish

267   *badges of these men:* Servants wore badges bearing their
        master's coat-of-arms to identify them as being in the
        service of their employer. Here, of course, Stephano and
        Trinculo are also wearing the clothing they found earlier and
        as such their "badges" show them as the rascals they are.

270-271 *make flows . . . power:* Sycorax could control the ebb and flow
        of the ties and use for her own purposes all the influence
        of the moon which could not resist her magic power.

279   *reeling ripe:* reeling drunk; i.e., staggering

280   *hath gilded 'em?:* drunk to the gills – a euphemism meaning
        extremely drunk or saturated with liquor up to the base of
        their throats

281   *in this pickle?:* in this wretched condition

282   *in such a pickle:* Trinculo is referring to the "wretched condi-
        tion" in which he found himself in the slimy pool.

284   *fly-blowing:* a reference to the process by which meat was
        pickled to keep it from too quickly becoming tainted

290   *disproportion'd:* misshapened, out of proportion

Trinculo: If these be true spies which I wear in my head,
    here's a goodly sight.   260
Caliban: O Setebos, these be brave spirits indeed!
    How fine my master is! I am afraid
    He will chastise me.
Sebastian: Ha, ha!
    What things are these, my lord Antonio?
    Will money buy 'em?
Antonio: Very like; one of them   265
    Is a plain fish, and, no doubt, marketable.
Prospero: Mark but the badges of these men, my lords,
    Then say if they be true. This mis-shapen knave,
    His mother was a witch; and one so strong
    That could control the moon, make flows and ebbs,   270
    And deal in her command, without her power.
    These three have robb'd me; and this demi-devil—
    For he's a bastard one—had plotted with them
    To take my life. Two of these fellows you
    Must know and own; this thing of darkness I   275
    Acknowledge mine.
Caliban: I shall be pinch'd to death.
Alonso: Is not this Stephano, my drunken butler?
Sebastian: He is drunk now: where had he wine?
Alonso: And Trinculo is reeling ripe: where should they
    Find this grand liquor that hath gilded 'em?—   280
    How camest thou in this pickle?
Trinculo: I have been in such a pickle, since I saw you last,
    that, I fear me, will never out of my bones: I shall
    not fear fly-blowing.
Sebastian: Why, how now, Stephano!   285
Stephano: O, touch me not;—I am not Stephano, but a
    cramp.
Prospero: You'd be king o' the isle, sirrah?
Stephano: I should have been a sore one, then.
Alonso: This is a strange thing as e'er I look'd on.
                        [Pointing to Caliban.]
Prospero: He is as disproportion'd in his manners   290
    As in his shape. Go, sirrah, to my cell;
    Take with you your companions; as you look
    To have my pardon, trim it handsomely.

298   *luggage:* the silly clothes which you have stolen

308   *nuptial:* the marriage ceremony

314-315 *auspicious gales/ . . . catch:* favourable winds which will pro-
        vide for you a voyage so swift that you will catch up with
        the rest of the fleet of ships in your party before it reaches
        Naples

Caliban: Ay, that I will; and I'll be wise hereafter,
    And seek for grace. What a thrice-double ass   295
    Was I, to take this drunkard for a god,
    And worship this dull fool!
Prospero: Go to; away!
Alonso: Hence, and bestow your luggage where you found
    it.
Sebastian: Or stole it, rather.
            [Exeunt Caliban, Stephano, and Trinculo.]
Prospero: Sir, I invite your Highness and your train   300
    To my poor cell, where you shall take your rest
    For this one night; which, part of it, I'll waste
    With such discourse as, I not doubt, shall make it
    Go quick away: the story of my life,
    And the particular incidents gone by   305
    Since I came to this isle; and in the morn
    I'll bring you to your ship, and so to Naples,
    Where I have hope to see the nuptial
    Of these our dear-beloved solemnized;
    And thence retire me to my Milan, where   310
    Every third thought shall be my grave.
Alonso: I long
    To hear the story of your life, which must
    Take the ear strangely.
Prospero: I'll deliver all;
    And promise you calm seas, auspicious gales,
    And sail so expeditious that shall catch   315
    Your royal fleet far off. *[Aside to Ariel.]* My Ariel, chick,
    That is thy charge: then to the elements
    Be free, and fare thou well! Please you, draw near.
                            [Exeunt.]

Epilogue.

Spoken by Prospero.

Now my charms are all o'erthrown,
And what strength I have's mine own,
Which is most faint: now, 'tis true,
I must be here confined by you,
Or sent to Naples. Let me not,   5
Since I have my dukedom got,
And pardon'd the deceiver, dwell
In this bare island by your spell;
But release me from my bands
With the help of your good hands: 10
Gentle breath of yours my sails
Must fill, or else my project fails,
Which was to please. Now I want
Spirits to enforce, art to enchant,
And my ending is despair,   15
Unless I be relieved by prayer,
Which pierces so that it assaults
Mercy itself, and frees all faults.
As you from crimes would pardon'd be,
Let your indulgence set me free.   20

Act 5, Scene 1: Activities

1. How would you stage the spell-stopped scene (lines 58–87). What effect would you want to create on an audience?
   Consider the following questions:
   - How would you have Prospero deliver his speech?
   - How would his listeners behave as they appeared before him?
   - What lighting and sound effects would you use?

   Rehearse the scene and present it to another group or to the class. Discuss the similarities and differences between the performances of different groups.

2. Other than a few final words, the last we hear from Ariel is his song, lines 88–94. Why do you think there are no farewell speeches between Prospero and Ariel?

   As a director, you feel that a formal farewell exchange between the two characters should be included. Write the speeches and insert them in an appropriate part of the scene.

3. a) Antonio and Sebastian don't have a lot to say in this final act. Reread the few comments they make and decide whether you think the two men feel any sorrow for their sins. Will they change as a result of their experience?

   b) As either Antonio or Sebastian, write a letter to a friend, explaining your feelings about the last night of your island adventure. Offer comments about what you plan to do when you return to Naples.

4. Reread Gonzalo's speech, lines 205–213, and explain in your own words what he is saying. With a partner, role-play an interview with Gonzalo, having him expand on the meaning of his speech.

Present this live interview to the rest of the class. Be prepared to respond to audience questions about the revelations and implications of his speech.

5. As Miranda, write the diary entry for this, your last night on the island. Reveal your feelings about leaving your home on the island to return to a city you left at age three. You might also include your thoughts about getting married and about referring to the future as "the brave new world".

6. With a partner discuss the content of Caliban's final speech, lines 294–297. Do you think he is sincere? How do you account for his change of heart? Write a prediction for Caliban. Will he stay on the island? Will he go with Prospero to Naples? In either case what will his life be like? Compare your prediction with others in your class.

7. When *The Tempest* is performed, frequently the epilogue is not included. Imagine that, as Shakespeare, you have just seen a production in which the epilogue was omitted. Write a letter to the director commenting on whether you think the director's choice was or was not a good one, and explaining why you think as you do.

   If possible find out what explanations have been given for not including the speech in verse by Prospero. Share your letter and your findings with classmates.

Consider the Whole Play

1. You have been hired by a publishing company to write a biography about Prospero, tentatively titled, *Prospero: His Life and Times.* You have been asked to submit a rough outline of the book, a tentative table of contents, an outline of each chapter, and a couple of paragraphs from the introduction and conclusion of your book. Create an outline that you would submit to the publisher. As you develop it, consider the possibility that it might be made into a movie at a later time.

2. Recall the two story lines that develop with the characters of Antonio and Sebastian and with Caliban, Trinculo, and Stephano. In two columns, list the parallels you observe between the story developments. Consider the following:
   - the personalities of the characters,
   - the objectives they have,
   - the strategies they decide on,
   - the setbacks they experience,
   - what finally happens to them.

   You might wish to perform highlights of both story lines. If so, prepare for your presentation by resolving the following questions:
   - What scenes or scene segments will you choose?
   - How will you stage your production so the audience understands the parallels you are developing?

   Present your performances to the class or make a video of them for class viewing.

3. Shakespeare's contemporary audiences lived in a time when the New World was being explored. Its potential for development triggered many and varied speculations within the social and economic communities in Europe about how native people could and should be treated by the explorers. Some critics believe that the way Caliban is treated in the play may reflect some of the ways explorers treated New World natives.

In a group discuss the extent to which you think *The Tempest* illustrates the conflict between "civilized" society and "natural" society. Use specific examples from the play to support your opinions. Which group in *The Tempest* do you think is the most civilized? Explain.

You might report your opinions by having one member from your group report to the class. You might prefer to write your thoughts in an essay to share with classmates.

4. Recall fairy tales you have read, seen performed, and/ or heard about. What are some of the elements common to most fairy tales? What elements in *The Tempest* remind you of the ingredients of a fairy tale?

Develop an outline for a fairy tale you could write based on *The Tempest*. Remember that many readers of fairy tales are young children. Keep your story simple. Decide where you will include illustrations and what other visual content they will have.

Discuss your outline with a partner, making any needed adjustments based on your partner's comments and recommendations.

Share a rough draft with a partner to obtain ideas for improving the content and/or style where necessary. Submit a second draft for editing and polishing the suggestions received. Prepare your illustrations and present your final product to the class. If appropriate, share your fairy tale with younger students for their comments.

5. A popular form of theatre in England during the late 16th and early 17th centuries was that of the *commedia dell'arte*. Using a library or resource centre, investigate this dramatic form. Locate information on aspects

of this form such as the following:
- stock characters,
- scenery,
- improvised dialogue.

In a group, present a short improvisation of a typical commedia dell'arte scenario, using a segment from *The Tempest*. You might use Stephano, Trinculo, and Caliban as the chief characters of your scene.

6. As a modern movie director of *The Tempest* consider how you will present either Caliban or Ariel to your audience. In a director's log make notes for the character you have selected on the following points:
   - the costume you will give your character
   - the make-up you will use
   - the special effects (sound, props) you will add to create the effect you want your audience to appreciate.
   Create a visual representation of the character with brief notes included to explain your character's presentation.

7. Create a poster advertising *The Tempest*. Before you begin, consider the following ideas:
   - What memorable line or lines might be the basis for the artwork?
   - Would you use any of the existing artwork? If so, which illustration(s) would you include?
   - Are there any quotes from the play that you might use?
   - Is there a segment of the play not already illustrated that you would include?
   Display your posters for the class to view.

8. Imagine that you are the planner hired to co-ordinate the wedding of Miranda and Ferdinand. What kind of celebration will you organize? To help you develop ideas, research Elizabethan wedding customs and

traditions. Decide the following:
- what kind of wedding invitation you will design
- the costumes the bride and groom will wear
- the number of people who will attend
- the food you will serve at the banquet
- the entertainment you will have
- what you will charge for your services.

Draft a statement that you would present to Prospero, outlining your plans and providing an estimate of the costs.

9. Compose a narrative piece of writing which presents your version of the play. Use the twelve illustrations included in this edition to help you create a picture book story of *The Tempest*. Share your story with the class and/or other interested audiences.

10. With others in a group, imagine that you are the characters en route to Milan. How might the people of Milan respond to you? What will you say to them? What decisions would you make in response to the following questions:
- Who will speak first? What initial statement will he/she make to the media?
- What questions from the media might you expect? What will your answers be?
- How do you think the first few days should be organized in order to re-establish order and control in Milan?

Select one member of your group to chair your planning meetings. Develop your strategies for your statements and actions when you return to Milan. Share your strategies with the rest of your class.

11. A production of *The Tempest* is scheduled to open next week in your community. As the host of a television show on your community network, you have been told to interview the director and two of the

actors in the play. Prepare an interview that will entice your television audience to buy tickets to a performance.

Decide what questions you should ask to encourage the show's viewers to see the play. With a partner, present the interview to classmates. At the end of the interview, see if your audience felt that your questions addressed the highlights of a production of *The Tempest*.

12. Choose one of the following debate propositions to use in an informal debate. Be it resolved that:
    • Gonzalo is a sentimental romantic rather than a wise and serious political advisor.
    • Caliban is by background and nature beyond redemption.
    • Miranda is an example of a naive and flirtatious adolescent.
    • Antonio is the kind of person with whom society must learn to live.

Form two teams of four members each and prepare arguments for either the *positive* position (agreeing with the debate proposition) or the *negative* position (disagreeing with the proposition). Students who are not members of the two teams could prepare questions to ask the team members at the end of the debate exchange. Questions for the debating teams should be directed to specific speakers.

At the conclusion of the debate share with the whole class your responses to the debate and the conclusions reached at the end of the debate.